Ethics in the Classroom

Bridging the Gap Between Theory and Practice

Dan Mahoney

ROWMAN & LITTLEFIELD EDUCATION
Lanham • *New York* • *Toronto* • *Plymouth, UK*

Published in the United States of America
by Rowman & Littlefield Education
A Division of Rowman & Littlefield Publishers, Inc.
A wholly owned subsidiary of The Rowman & Littlefield Publishing Group, Inc.
4501 Forbes Boulevard, Suite 200, Lanham, Maryland 20706
www.rowmaneducation.com

Estover Road
Plymouth PL6 7PY
United Kingdom

British Library Cataloguing in Publication Information Available

Library of Congress Cataloging-in-Publication Data
Mahoney, Dan, 1940-
  Ethics in the classroom : bridging the gap between theory and practice /
Dan Mahoney.
      p. cm.
  Includes bibliographical references.
  ISBN-13: 978-1-57886-767-7 (cloth : alk. paper)
  ISBN-10: 1-57886-767-3 (cloth : alk. paper)
  ISBN-13: 978-1-57886-768-4 (pbk. : alk. paper)
  ISBN-10: 1-57886-768-1 (pbk. : alk. paper)
  1. Teachers—Professional ethics. 2. Teaching—Moral and ethical
aspects. I. Title.
  LB1779.M35 2008
  174.'93711--dc22

                                                    2007042969

⊗™ The paper used in this publication meets the minimum requirements of
American National Standard for Information Sciences—Permanence of Paper
for Printed Library Materials, ANSI/NISO Z39.48-1992.
Manufactured in the United States of America

For Erin and Kelsey

Contents

Preface

Perhaps you are browsing through this book at a conference or a bookstore. Perhaps you are looking through it for the first time in one of your courses. Whether you are a teacher, or studying to be a teacher, this book is for you.

This book is for you because several years ago I set out to understand one of the most perplexing dynamics I experienced repeatedly in the K–12 school system: the pervasive presence of ethically compromising situations. The first few times I experienced them, I chalked them up to individual personalities, the inability to speak truth to power, or simply poor communication. But when I began to see the near-constant presence of ethically compromising situations over the years, and in a variety of settings, I began to suspect that there was a lot more going on than just some personality issues here or poor communication there; I began to suspect that there was something inherent in the complex interpersonal dynamics, in the individual notions of professional practice, or in the organizations themselves, to make such a thing so pervasive. I also began to realize that nowhere in our training as educators were we prepared for such troubling situations or how to deal with them.

So, after moving from the K–12 environment to the university environment, where our work is not only to teach but also to research and create new knowledge, I set out to understand this phenomenon. What you have in your hands is the result of that search.

In this book you will read examples of teachers caught in the daily reality of ethically compromising situations that occur due to a complex array of organizational demands upon, and interpersonal dynamics among, people who are sincerely committed to helping their students and colleagues achieve the greater good. You will read about teachers who don't want to use deception but who also acknowledge that often they must in order to meet the needs of their students. You will read about how the teacher's role of protecting the interests of students often conflicts with the rules of the organization or, perhaps, their own best interests. In such situations, ethical complexity is guaranteed.

When I began my study of the practical and professional ethics of educators, I simply wanted to understand how they made sense of the ethically complex situations in which they found themselves, and how they managed the situations in their professional practice. Now, years later, I know this topic holds a great deal of importance as an in-service and pre-service training issue. Consequently, this book speaks to educators in their pre-service and in-service years, and it should be of particular interest to people who work with teachers in courses of professional and practical ethics.

In addition to a tour of various ethical decision-making perspectives, the tales in this book weave together aspects of people's emotional make-up, they way they think, their past experiences, and their hopes and desires for the future. These composites of people in real situations tell stories of how ordinary teachers in ordinary circumstances face all manner of complexities in their work, from issues of confidentiality and inappropriate relationships to issues of school policy and moral obligations.

This is a book about the role of ethics in helping teachers function more effectively with the interpersonal and organizational complexities in schools. It presents an array of theoretical and practical perspectives to enhance our comprehension of the ethical complexities that come into play in the schoolhouse.

The composite case studies in this book not only describe individual's current professional ethics, they make an important contribution to individuals who desire to _improve_ their functioning in ethically complex situations.

In short, this book tells the story of real people caught in difficult situations—and therefore provides a revealing, honest, and practical examination of the practical and professional ethics of educators.

I am hopeful that you will read this book and find affirmation and validation in its theoretical grounding, in the people you meet in its pages, and in the enormity of the task of teaching students and running schools. I hope that teachers, teachers in training, and students in educational ethics programs see in this book the integrity of its scholarship, its authenticity of describing the realities of professional practice, and its promise for promoting lively discussions and enhanced professional practice.

I also hope that you will find in this book some catalyst for introspection and personal growth. During the 15 years I have taught and worked with graduate students, all of whom are working teachers and principals, I had the privilege of learning from them and of asking myself about my own professional ethics. Talking with these brave and generous people has helped me reflect on how to be a better human being in complex organizations in a confusing world. I wish the same for you.

Acknowledgments

I wish to dispel the myth that academic research and writing is carried out in isolation, and I give thanks to all of the people who helped in so many ways throughout the conceptualization, writing, and completion of this book.

My colleagues at Gonzaga University continue to inspire and guide my thinking and work in many ways. Our wonderfully rich conversations in hallways, airports, and on the road provide some of the best professional development possible.

I thank Al Fein for our constant and on-going conversation about ethics, leadership, improving the functioning of schools, and caring for the people who study and work in them. His vantage point as a veteran school administrator and university professor, and our many conversations about this topic, have helped more than he knows.

The adult students in my graduate ethics classes have been indispensable in the continued examination of the practical and professional ethics of educators. Thanks are also due to those courageous teachers and administrators who have confided their deepest concerns and troubling situations for your benefit. Their daily effort on behalf of their students, while faced with limited resources, political pressures, interpersonal conflicts, complex family dynamics, and conflicting demands, make them the backbone of our school system. Their courage and honesty in describing the ethical compromises they are forced to deal with makes them the heroes of this book. Thank you, one and all. I treasure you and our time together.

I thank one and all for your expertise, your attention to detail, and your help in making this book better than it would have been without your help.

I thank my wife, Scooter, for her constant generosity, good cheer, and assistance in this, and every, endeavor.

1

Introduction

> There is something in all of us that loves to put together a puzzle, that loves to see the image of the whole emerge. The beauty of a person, or a flower, or a poem lies in seeing all of it.
>
> Peter Senge

What are people really like? What makes people operate the way they do? What happens when people face difficult options and do things they do not believe in? Examining ourselves—why we do what we do—is the very essence of human psychology—and of ethics. The study of ethics, from the work of Plato 2,400 years ago to the more contemporary work of Downie and Telfer, constitutes a rich tradition in both human psychology and philosophy.

The purpose of this text on ethical decision making is not to illustrate the difference between right and wrong, but to show how teachers might choose among ethical approaches to decision making as they face the difficult choices they must make every day. When classroom teachers face difficult and ethically complex situations, it is not always a simple task to weigh the issues of right and wrong, of ethics and justice. Most of us like to think of ourselves as just and ethical people. However, to be just and ethical, people need to know something about the demands of justice and how they apply in our own circumstances. What is fair? What is just? How do we decide? These are the central concerns of the ethical theorists presented in the following chapters.

The next seven chapters present seven major theories of ethics in preparation for applying them to the types of ethically complex situations that teachers experience in their professional practice. The seven theorists are: Plato, David Hume, Immanuel Kant, John Stuart Mill, Ayn Rand, Mohandas Gandhi, and the joint work of R. S. Downie and Elizabeth Telfer.

I chose these seven perspectives for four reasons. First, each of these theorists makes a significant contribution to, and represents a distinctly different position in, the continuum of ethical theory from the tradition of Western philosophy. Second, these seven perspectives of ethics form an identifiable core of the Western tradition of philosophy and ethics. Third, they present a broad historical overview of the development of ethical theory. Finally, these seven theories represent a continuum of ethical decision-making typologies that can be used to identify the manner in which educators make ethical decisions.

None of these philosophers spoke specifically about the ethically complex situations that schoolteachers face, such as the interpersonal dynamics of working in large, nonheterogeneous staffs, the pressures created by political dynamics, the personality-based problems inherent in supervisory roles, or the professional ethics of other teachers. None of these philosophers spoke directly to the issues of managing a behavioral contract with a student, or about the complexities of interacting with less-than-supportive parents, or about which students should be exempted from standardized tests, or about accounting for differences in student conduct. None of these ethical theorists spoke directly to the issue of dealing with negative cultural norms, the subtle messages from mentors, or the quid pro quo agreements between the office, the secretary, and just *some* of the teachers. What they did speak to, however, are the basic concepts that have proven to be exceptionally valuable in considering such complex situations: justice, sentiment, reason, benefits, and respect.

In preparing to apply these various theories of ethical decision making to the complex array of situations that teachers face, it is helpful to understand that the term *ethics* often refers to the study of values concerning how people choose to live. In the formal study of ethics, the term is often used interchangeably with moral philosophy. When ethics is considered apart from formal studies in philosophy, it refers to common-sense behavior, acceptable behavior, or acceptable rules of conduct.

Common-sense behavior, for purposes of this text, may be defined as those unwritten judgments that schoolteachers and principals are forced to make within the constraints of their work with students and their middle-management positions. School principals, in the process of their middle-management positions, make hundreds of such common-sense judgments every year; classroom teachers make even more.

Clarification of terms relating to the discussion of ethical decision making is appropriate before proceeding too far with this material. Following are the definitions of five terms used in this text:

1. *Ethos* refers to the distinguishing character or guiding beliefs of a person or a group, and can be witnessed by what the person or group does.
2. *Ethic*, or *ethics*, refers to the principles of conduct governing an individual or a group. As mentioned above, the term ethics can also refer to a systematic study of those principles of conduct.
3. *Ethical* suggests the involvement of more difficult or subtle questions of just, fair, or equitable behavior in accordance with accepted standards of conduct.
4. *Moral* implies conformity to established sanctioned codes or accepted standards of behavior considered to be good. The ethics of a person or a group make up the formula from which moral conduct follows.
5. *Morality* is simply the practice of ethical behavior in conformity with established norms of what is considered to be good. Morality is the conduct that follows from one's ethical base.

GOALS OF THE BOOK

Of all the humanistic disciplines, ethics is the one that deals directly with the human experience of how we live and how we think we should live. What happens when we face difficult options and do things we do not believe in? This examination of who we are as a people invariably becomes an examination of who we are as individuals. This examination helps us go beyond the families and schools of our own traditions and become aware of the experiences of others.

A major purpose of this book is to encourage you to question and challenge the decisions and judgments that you, as a schoolteacher, make within the constraints of your work and in the context of your formal and informal roles with students, teachers, and parents.

Another purpose of this text is to illustrate how schoolteachers might recognize their biases and predispositions and choose among ethical approaches to decision making as they face the hard choices of their profession. Through presentation and critique of theory and of professional practice, users of this text will be able to establish a broader picture of the forces that affect ethical decision making, relate what they have learned to their own professional practice, and refine personal principles of ethical decision making. Accordingly, the major goals are for you, as a user of this book, to:

1. Increase your understanding of the forces that affect your ethical decision making.
2. Examine your experiences regarding the impact of others' ethical decision making.

3. Examine your ethical decision making regarding its impact on others.
4. Practice discernment of ethically compromising situations.
5. Increase your understanding of a variety of divergent frameworks of ethical decision making and how such frameworks might affect your decision making with regard to your students and your colleagues.
6. Apply your enhanced ethical decision making to your professional environment.

SAMPLE LEARNING ACTIVITIES

Presented next are several learning activities that are designed to support you in using and learning this material. As you work your way through the text and work on these learning activities, I encourage you to consider the point that participation in discussions about the case studies in this book and the ethically complex situations behind them is essential. Part of developing a full understanding of this material is listening to, considering, and understanding issues and opinions from different points of view. Your involvement in such discussions is an important dimension of the design of this text. To put it another way, you have things to teach that others could not learn without you.

Sample Learning Activity #1: Description of Ethical Compromise

Write a 3- to 5-page description of a school-based situation in which you felt some degree of ethical compromise or a situation in which you felt some doubt about the ethical issues involved. In this learning activity, do the following five things:

1. Describe the situation.
2. Describe your emotional response.
3. Describe your intellectual response.
4. Describe your actual actions.
5. Describe the forces that affected the situation.

Limit your description to a situation that occurred in relation to your professional life, areas such as personnel issues, policy and procedure, testing, legal confidentiality, budget and finances, ethnicity, gender, personal privacy, other policies and procedures, curricular integrity, and relationships with colleagues, students, parents, or community. You will see examples of this approach in the case studies in this book.

Sample Learning Activity #2: New Description of Ethical Compromise

Belief statements and descriptions of personal philosophies are all grand and noble things. Such statements, however, tend to represent our highest ideals, not our daily practice. Too often, in the grind of real and personal political human interaction, our ability to remember or access those ideals is strained. Something that can be more valuable than describing the highest rung on the ladder is simply to reach for and describe the next rung up on the ladder. Therefore, rather than compose a description of your personal philosophy of ethical decision making, do the following: In order to further apply your knowledge of theories of ethical decision making, write a 3- to 5-page description of a more recent school-based situation (different from the one you described for the first learning activity) in which you felt some degree of ethical compromise or a situation in which you felt some doubt about the ethical issues involved. For this learning activity, do six things:

1. As before, describe the situation.
2. As before, describe your emotional response.
3. As before, describe your intellectual response.
4. As before, describe your actual actions.
5. As before, describe the forces that affected the situation.
6. In this learning activity, however, describe your new insights, your emotional responses that might be different in some way, the differences in your intellectual responses, the differences in your actual actions, and any new or different awareness of the forces that affected the situation as a result of your involvement with any of the material presented in this course via the lectures, readings in the text, role plays, or discussions in class.

Sample Learning Activity #3: Analysis of Ethical Decision Making

Write a 3- to 5-page formal analysis or critique of your ethical decision making in your professional life, making use of any of the material presented in this course via the lectures, readings in the text, role plays, or discussions in class. You will see an example of this type of approach in Chapter 20.

Sample Learning Activity #4: Ethics Learning Activity Project

Individually or in a small group, create a multidimensional and interactive game that appropriately involves students at your grade level(s) in the content and concepts presented in this course.

Sample Learning Activity #5: Personal Ethics Journal

Through your professional interactions and through other experiences, you might have found an aspect or two of current educational practice that you simply cannot ethically support. Use what you are learning from your reading, your writing, and the class presentations and discussions to analyze and critique those practices you find ethically compromising. Keep an ongoing journal of those workplace situations you find to be ethically compromising. In your journal, describe the situations, your emotional responses, your intellectual responses, your actions, the forces that affected the situations, and your insights as they develop. Document the interventions you make and describe their effects. To the degree that makes sense, relate your descriptions to the course material. Present your journal in whatever format makes the most sense for you.

Sample Learning Activity #6: Ethics Curriculum Project

Create an individual or collaborative presentation of a Curriculum Improvement Plan that focuses on ethics at your grade levels. This plan should include the basics of curricular design—identification or revision of goals, adoption of new materials, an implementation plan for a new program or materials, identifying assessment procedures, and so on. Completion of this curriculum project should demonstrate inclusion of the major elements that are included in this book.

Sample Learning Activity #7: Conference Presentation on Ethics

Create a 45-minute presentation, complete with the appropriate use of technology (PowerPoint/DVD/video, for example) or other appropriate media (psychodrama, role play, for example), suitable for presentation at a regional or national conference having to do with ethics or the curricular integration of ethics, in your subject area and grade level.

Sample Learning Activity #8: Personal Reflection

Gandhi once told a person who asked for help in making decisions: "I will give you a talisman. Whenever you are in doubt about an action, apply the following test: recall the face of the poorest and weakest man you have seen, and ask yourself if the step you contemplate is going to be of any use to him. Will he gain anything by it? Will it restore him to a control over his own life and destiny?" (Nair, 1997, pp. 117–118.)

Describe a school-based situation about which you sensed some ethical complexity. Recall the face of the least powerful or least well-served person in that situation. Then, describe who benefited the most and who benefited the least. Finally, ask yourself, if there could have been a better outcome, what would it have been? How could you have helped to bring it about?

Sample Learning Activity #9: Reflection and Discussion Questions

Each chapter is followed by an array of reflection and discussion questions that ask you to consider the issues, the ethical dimensions of the case, and the deeper practical and professional ethics of teachers. For example:

1. Do teachers have an ethical obligation to teach whatever curriculum the school, district, or state requires if they find the content to be questionable, inaccurate, or offensive?
2. What kind of ethical compromises might be created by "teaching the students, not the curriculum"?
3. Do teachers who are also parents have greater ethical responsibilities toward their own children than toward their colleagues?

These are examples of the issues that all teachers, new and highly experienced, face every year. Your work as a teacher will be that much more ethically grounded by your deep involvement in discussing these issues.

Sample Learning Activity #10: Service to Others

The *Golden Rule* is to treat others as ourselves. Without the compass of absolute values, among which is service to others, what instrument do we have to guide ourselves? Whether we are teachers, department heads, principals, or superintendents, the principle remains the same: We serve our fellow human beings because it is the right thing to do. We do not have to wait for a great cause to make a personal commitment to personal service; it can start with those nearest to us: our students. Personal service leads to a shared experience, which creates the deepest understanding and the most lasting bonds of attachment. What can you do to be of service to others?

SUMMARY

As stated earlier, most of us like to think of ourselves as just and ethical people. But to be just and ethical, we need to know something about the demands of justice and ethics and how they apply in our own circumstances. Another way to say this is that we cannot talk about ethics without talking about *ethics*, and that is what this book is for. In order to answer the questions, "What is fair? What is just? How do we decide?" we have to read, understand, and know about these central concerns from an array of ethical perspectives. The next seven chapters present such an array.

The next seven chapters, each of which represents a distinctly different position in the continuum of ethical theory from the tradition of Western philosophy, give you the background knowledge you will need to question and challenge the decisions and judgments that you, as a teacher, make within the constraints of your work and in the context of your formal and informal roles with students, teachers, and parents. Then, the reflection and discussion questions will help you relate what you have learned to your own professional practice and to refine your personal principles of ethical decision making.

REFLECTION AND DISCUSSION QUESTIONS

1. What kind of background knowledge do you have about any of these seven philosophers?
2. Can you state some examples of the differences between ethical issues and moral issues?
3. Describe the ethos of different schools you've attended or in which you have worked.
4. Describe some of the characteristics of a person you already know and admire.

2

Due Process of the Law

Doing what is unjust is far worse than suffering it.

Plato

Because the concept of justice is central to most theories of ethics, we begin with Plato's work, in which he develops a definition of justice and places it directly in the center of his framework of ethical decision making.

Plato was deeply concerned with justice, especially as it relates to decisions made by leaders. Plato defined the concept several ways in *Plato's Republic* (380 BC/1974), ranging from "justice is to perform one's own task and not to meddle with that of others" (p. 98), to "justice does not lie in a man's external actions, but in the way he acts within himself. He does not allow his soul to meddle with another" (p. 107). In *Gorgias* (385 BC/1987), Plato talks about justice in a manner approximating a contemporary legal definition: "Justice: Proper administration of laws. In jurisprudence, the constant and perpetual disposition of legal matters or disputes to render every man his due" (Black, 1991, p. 599).

For the purposes of this chapter, then, justice can be defined as "right conduct toward others through due process of the law." This definition encompasses doing one's own work, not meddling with the work of others, and ensuring that every person is appropriately recognized and compensated.

In *Gorgias*, Plato contended that the pursuit of justice is most admirable because it provides "either the most pleasure, or benefit, or both" (385 BC/ 1987, p. 46), and that "what a man should guard himself against most of all is doing what's unjust" (p. 49). Plato also argued that education and justice are the primary determinants of happiness.

Regarding the pursuit of justice, Plato believed that one should know justice before practicing leadership, so as not to say things merely to please the crowds. Plato believed the craft of caring for the soul was the most important of all, and that true leaders had the responsibility of practicing that craft. The craft of caring for the soul could not be practiced without the knowledge of justice.

Looking further into his work as it relates to right action and the use of power, Plato wrote, "If a person does anything for the sake of something, he doesn't want this thing that he's doing, but the thing for the *sake* of which he's doing it" (p. 29). From this position, he maintained that if a just person were to punish another justly, that punishment was done because it was a good thing, a better thing to do than to not do. Plato then asserted that committing an unjust act is a greater evil than being treated unjustly: "So, because it surpasses it in evil, doing what's unjust would be more evil than suffering it. Injustice, then . . . and all other forms of corruption of soul are the greatest evil there is" (pp. 33–45).

Plato spelled out his definition of *unjust* very clearly in *Plato's Republic*: "We have shown that it is never just to harm anyone" (380BC/1974, p. 10). Thus, if an action harms someone, it is unjust. Plato also stated in his *Republic* that injustice makes an individual incapable of achievement because he is at odds within himself and is not of one mind; he further notes that injustice makes any organization incapable of achieving anything.

It is important to note that in *Gorgias* (385 BC/1987), Plato asserted that all forms of corporal and capital punishment, sentenced justly, as authorized by law as punishment for unjust behavior, would be just punishments carried out for the benefit of the person. Plato, the idealist, believed that pain and suffering were the only ways "to get rid of injustice" (p. 109), and that one's soul undergoes improvement if he is justly disciplined.

Plato believed that there are corrupt conditions of the soul and named among them cowardice, ignorance, injustice, and lack of discipline. He argued that injustice and doing what is unjust are the greatest evils, and that paying a debt for them is what gets rid of the evil. Plato believed that the full and proper administration of justice, in that it gets rid of injustice and poor discipline, is the greatest benefit of all.

Through this analysis of Plato's theory, justice can be defined as right conduct toward others through due process of the law. Any action of a person that causes harm to another person, therefore, can be labeled unjust. Committing the evil of injustice makes individuals and organizations incapable of achieving anything worthwhile. Finally, one must pay for, or be punished for, the evil of committing an unjust act.

PLATO'S ETHICS AND THE CASE STUDIES

In applying Plato's theory to the case studies presented later in this book, it is important to point out that schools, teachers, and school administrators, are governed by local, state, and federal laws. Any violation of these laws or of local school or district rules, standards, or principles would be considered by Plato to be unjust. Among the laws teachers and school administrators are responsible for upholding, is one in which the state asserts the right to intervene in order to safeguard the general welfare of children. In this law, provisions are made for the reporting of information to appropriate public authorities about cases of neglect and abuse of children. It identifies all people required to report actual or suspected instances of child abuse, which includes institutional personnel. Any violation of this law generally constitutes a misdemeanor.

Clearly, Plato would hold that all school personnel are obligated to carry out all legal requirements. If teachers were willing to violate administrative and civil law for the purpose of what would appear to be protecting their own interests, they would be hurting other people and perpetuating a system that harmed both the people in it and the people it intended to serve. Plato would hold that such teachers would be acting out of cowardice, and that they would be serving their own interests of position over their responsibility of justice and due process toward others, the students. Plato would maintain that ignoring due process hurts innocent people, that doing so to protect personal interests is unethical and a great evil, and that it would result in the person, or perhaps the organization, being "incapable of achieving anything" as a unit.

SUMMARY OF PLATO'S ETHICS

From Plato's arguments in *Gorgias* and his *Republic*, five key components of his theory of ethics, especially as they relate to teachers' ethical dilemmas presented in the case studies, can be identified:

1. Justice can be defined as the "right conduct toward others through due process of the law."
2. Any action a person takes that causes harm to another person can be identified and labeled as unjust and unethical.
3. Doing an unjust act is evil and unethical.
4. Injustice on the part of individuals or organizations makes them incapable of achieving anything.
5. Individuals must pay for, or be punished for, the evil of doing an unjust act.

Plato believed that the quest for truth and justice is critically important. Plato's theory supports the pursuit of what is best for everybody and that "what is best for everybody" is comprised of right conduct toward others, for without attention paid to right conduct toward others, life becomes a scramble for limited resources, with only a few in control.

Plato held that to do an injustice to another person is a great evil and that it damages one's own soul, as well. One point of Plato's theory, that no good can come from the professional practice of one who does unjust things, supports the notion that unjust acts move individuals and organizations toward corruption. Once people—teachers, in this case—start hiding evidence of wrongdoing, where do they stop? Once teachers believe they have a choice about whether or not to follow the law, who decides which laws to uphold or when to uphold them? What message would such actions send to the students?

Plato's idealist arguments about absolute truth and justice are, simply put, the thin line between totalitarianism and anarchy. Are they applicable to the practical and professional ethics of schoolteachers? Plato's theory of ethics might well be paraphrased: The quest for ultimate truth and justice is a worthy and necessary pursuit, because in the end, without it, anything goes.

REFLECTION AND DISCUSSION QUESTIONS

1. Justice can be defined as the "right conduct toward others through due process of the law," which encompasses doing one's own work and not meddling with the work of others. Describe a situation in which someone has "meddled" with you and your work.
2. Describe an action through which a person has harmed you.
3. Describe an action that you have taken that caused harm to someone else. What caused you to do it? What were the results?
4. What do you think of the idea that injustice on the part of individuals or organizations makes them incapable of achieving anything? Describe some examples.
5. What do you think of Plato's idea that individuals must pay for, or be punished for, the evil of doing an unjust act? Compare "getting away with" an unjust act to "getting punished for" an unjust act. What did you learn from the experiences?
6. Describe someone in your life who is like Plato.
7. Describe why you would, or would not, like to work for a principal who ascribed to Plato's ethics.
8. What are the strengths and weaknesses of Plato's ethics in the pre-K–12 environment?

9. Does the fact that a specific activity is illegal always mean that it is also unethical? Give some examples of why or why not.
10. Does the fact that a specific activity is legal always mean that it is also ethical? Give some examples.
11. If specific activities were legal on one side of a city/county/state/national border, but illegal on the other side of that border, how would that affect the ethicality of the activities?
12. We can look back and see that we have engaged in all sorts of injustices to people that were condoned by the law, at the time. Describe some things we are currently doing that you think we will someday question the ethics of doing.

3

Utility and Agreeableness

Truth is disputable; not taste.

David Hume

The Scottish philosopher, David Hume, attempted to show that utility and agreeableness, and nothing else, are the values at the root of ethics. In his *An Enquiry Concerning the Principles of Morals* (1751/1983), Hume argued that ethical judgments are really judgments about what people consider to be virtues and vices, and that ethical judgments can be derived through observation of what *is*—through the observation of what people do and what they value.

Hume's theory is sentiment-based and, therefore, denies that there are any ethical facts. He wrote, "Truth is disputable; not taste. What exists in the nature of things is the standard of our judgment; what each man feels within himself is the standard of sentiment" (p. 14). Hume defines virtue to be "whatever mental action or quality gives to a spectator the pleasing sentiment of approbation; and vice the contrary" (p. 85). Hume wouldn't necessarily condemn any particular action; the same action might be wrong in one situation and acceptable in another. This is what constitutes the "flexibility" in Hume's theory of ethics.

Hume listed virtues that he believed every culture valued. Among these was self-interest, which Hume argued is both a valuable part of nature and compatible with interest in others. Building on this idea, he came up with the notion of "enlightened" self-interest, meaning that one does not pursue one's interest to the detriment of others. Hume presupposes that justice is based on community moral values, and that it must emerge out of shared community values.

To Hume, *utility* is the sole origin of ethical behavior and justice. He explained, "The rules of behavior and justice depend entirely on the particular state and condition in which men are placed and owe their origin and existence to that utility, which results to the public from their strict and regular observance" (p. 23).

Hume equated justice with the way people relate to one another regarding property rights, with "property" meaning real property and "social goods" as well. Regarding the practice of justice, the regulation of property or social goods, he explained, "We must be acquainted with the nature and situation of man, must reject appearances, which may be false, though specious, and must search for those rules, which are, on the whole, most useful and beneficial" (p. 28).

Hume argued that one's obligation to obey laws is founded on nothing but the interests of society. He also held that the various consequences of any practice are, on many occasions, doubtful and subject to inquiry. Hume believed that the object of municipal laws is to fix all of these questions with regard to justice, and that an accurate sense of judgment is often required to give the true determination "amidst such intricate doubts arising from obscure or opposite utilities" (p. 83).

Hume believed that justice is absolutely requisite to the well-being of mankind and the existence of society. Regarding the virtue of justice, Hume argued that the benefit resulting from it is not the consequence of every single act, but, rather, arises from the consequence for the greater part of society.

HUME'S ETHICS AND THE CASE STUDIES

As Hume proposes, the practice of justice is the search for the most useful and beneficial rules for society, and that people are obligated to promote society's best interests. Although serving one's self-interest is not wrong, it should not take place at the expense of other people.

Hume believed in the practical application of reason. He believed that sentiment, or feelings, provided the goals, but he also believed that reason and judgment help people reach those goals. Regarding the upcoming case studies, Hume would acknowledge that "obscure and opposite utilities, various interests" are seemingly at play and that "an accurate sense of reason or judgment is often required" to manage this issue.

Regarding the ethically complex situations faced by schoolteachers, concerns arise as to how to handle the various situations from Hume's theory of ethics. The appropriate behavior of all staff members in a school is one issue; the safety and well-being of all students in their care is another. Having staff members display appropriate modeling for the students is a third issue. Hume might argue, in some cases, that for teachers to choose not to follow some rules, laws, or policies, might be to act in disregard for the best interests of society.

Hume could contend that a specific illegal activity might not be of great concern under certain circumstances. For example: Suppose a high schoolteacher and his senior-year student were in love with each other; suppose they planned to marry once she turned 18. Would justice be served in making an issue out of the situation? Here could be a situation that is not terribly threatening to society's laws in which the need for legal intervention might not be so great. In words indicative of a Humean response, "It depends."

Hume identified a host of virtues that he claimed people hold dear and use to blame or judge people and their actions. Among them are justice and courage.

Also among them are norms of professional ethical behavior. Teachers clearly have the obligation to put the needs of their students first. If teachers carry out these responsibilities, they will have demonstrated the pursuit of justice and demonstrated the virtues of discretion and prudence. If teachers fail to carry out their obligations, what lack of moral virtues do they fail to display? A few come to mind: justice, honor, and courage. Hume acknowledged that various outcomes and utilities are difficult to sort out; he does, however, offer a clear picture of teachers' moral obligations.

SUMMARY OF HUME'S ETHICS

Hume believed that people's emotion determines their goals, and that rationality helps people achieve their goals. This last point separates Hume from other earlier philosophers who held a deep-seated distrust of human emotions. Hume believed that benevolence spans cultures and that no one would deliberately hurt another. His theory, however, is based on his assumptions, his generalizations, and his interpretation of his observations, and he trusted that it all fell into a good schema. It is possible that some of Hume's assumptions lack an internal consistency and that some of his generalizations are incorrect.

Hume acknowledged the difficulty of weighing the various utilities and outcomes inherent in many situations. He expressed an innate trust in people's ability to use their reasoning and judgment to sort things out. In many instances, however, the outcomes of actions are beyond the ability of mankind to reason out ahead of time. People do not always know where their actions will lead, so it is in the best interest of all people to act with regard to future generations, not just present-day society.

Regarding the case studies, would it be permissible to ignore a teacher's problematic behavior if his intentions were honorable and aimed at serving his interpretation of students' needs? Would it be less permissible to ignore the same problematic behavior if the intentions were based on self-interest? Might ignoring a teacher's problematic behavior prove to be correct regardless of the laws and consequences? Might ignoring a teacher's problematic behavior prove to be correct if everything eventually turned out okay?

Such a concern for the future implies a system of moral behavior that goes beyond the immediate pleasure or displeasure provided to society. Were we able to trace some current problem back to an action of an earlier time and then travel to that time to make the displeasing outcome known to the one who acted, would we be able to claim the act to be an immoral one? If not, why not? Would Hume claim a statute of limitations on the morality or immorality of actions? If so, what is it?

These questions make it difficult to disregard the timetable question of outcome-based ethics. When people consider their "greater happiness," do they consider just their circle of friends or do they extend their consideration to their city? Do they stop at their city or do they extend their consideration to the nation or the world? Do they cease their considerations with their generation or extend them to future generations?

This issue of the timetable of outcomes as measures of ethicality of actions is a difficult one to make sense of or respond to in a time-based reality. It is, at best, unclear whether Hume gave adequate attention to the "greater happiness" of society. He argued: "While we are ignorant, whether a man were aggressor or not, how can we determine whether the person who killed him, be criminal or innocent? But after every circumstance, every relation is known; the understanding has no farther room to operate. . . . The approbation or blame, which then ensues, cannot be the work of the judgment, but of the heart" (p. 85).

If people limit their approbation or blame, if people limit their "work of the heart" to only the present, do they not then disregard the past and fail to learn from it? If people fail to learn from the past, do they not then fail to grow more sensitive to the greater happiness of society? And do they not then fail to make any consideration for the well-being of society in the future? An internally consistent interpretation of Hume's theory of ethics could present a vision of a self-shaping society spiraling into collective disregard for anything outside of its sense of its own greater happiness. This concern for a bias-free perspective implies some system of moral behavior that goes beyond the immediate pleasure or displeasure provided to society.

In freeing himself from the heavy-handed religious authoritarianism of his day and making use of the trend of scientific observation, Hume created a system for examining the ethicality of individuals' decisions and actions. A troubling aspect of Hume's theory is that an action might be ethically acceptable in some situations, but not in others.

Some of the reasoning and application of Hume's theory is practical. Ethically complex school-based situations do exist in which, once all the evidence has been gathered, a person's behavior can be seen to be free of malice or the result of ignorance and misunderstanding. The very same act committed by one who did it with the intent to harm another can be a more serious situation. What becomes evident, from this example, is that the appropriate application of Hume's theory requires a person to act from a position of reason and experience, a well-seasoned professional practice.

Another troubling aspect of Hume's theory is his belief that the ethicality of a decision is based on its outcomes, which may not be known for years. To compound this problem, the outcomes may vary at different times. People's sentiments regarding an action and its outcome may vary widely for years after a decision has been made.

Because people cannot always see to the end of their actions, they must act with prudence and a positive regard for the future. This is the use of reason and compassion, and a high moral regard for more than mere convenience or present-day utility. Hume's theory argues that society, indeed, shapes itself toward what he holds to be universally valued virtues.

If one sees society's perceptions of benefits to society as culturally and temporally bound, and, therefore, not adequate measures of morality, Hume's ideas become problematic. His theory is perhaps most useful as a description of how he believes people *do* make moral decisions, not a philosophy of how people *should* make moral decisions. In this regard, his theory offers little in the way of providing immediate guidance for the difficult decisions teachers must make in ethically complex school-based situations that are, more often than not, bound by some type of immediate or local policy or law. Hume's description of the way people do make difficult decisions is, however, appropriate for self-examination. Hume's description of the ways people make difficult decisions is also helpful for questioning our broader professional practice and the applicability of the laws to which we are bound. Finally, Hume's description of the ways people make difficult decisions is also helpful in understanding why some teachers might choose to engage in hard-to-understand professional behavior.

REFLECTION AND DISCUSSION QUESTIONS

1. Hume defines virtue to be "whatever mental action or quality gives to a spectator the pleasing sentiment of approbation, and vice the contrary." What do you think of this definition of virtue?
2. Hume wouldn't necessarily condemn any particular action; the same action might be wrong in one situation and acceptable in another. What do you think of this flexibility in Hume's theory of ethics?

3. If the ethicality of a decision is based on its outcomes, which ultimately may not be known for years, when do we make such a decision?

4. Describe something you have done that was acceptable in one situation, but would be wrong in another.

5. Describe some examples in which the same action in a pre-K–12 environment might be wrong in one situation, yet acceptable in another.

6. In terms of school-based rules and consequences, what do you think of the idea that once all the evidence has been gathered, a student's or a teacher's behavior can be seen to be free of malice or the result of ignorance and misunderstanding, and that the very same act committed by one who did it with the intent to harm another can be a more serious situation?

7. What do you think of the aspect of Hume's theory that the ethicality of a decision is based on its outcomes, which may not be known for years? Describe some examples.

8. Hume says truth is disputable; not taste. What are your thoughts about this statement?

9. What might Plato and Hume say about the ethics of suicide?

10. Describe someone in your life who is like Hume.

11. Describe why you would, or would not, like to work for a principal who ascribed to Hume's ethics.

12. What do you think the strengths and weaknesses of Hume's ethics are in the pre-K–12 environment?

13. Compare and contrast Plato's ethics and Hume's ethics with regard to any issue in the school environment. For example:
   - Seeing a student in the process of cheating on a math exam.
   - Knowing of teachers giving extra time to students in timed exams.
   - Wearing hats in class.
   - Throwing snowballs at recess.
   - Knowing of an educator who occasionally smokes marijuana at home.
   - Knowing of a student who gets hit at home.
   - Knowing of a romance between an 18-year-old student and a 22-year-old teacher.
   - Selling coffee and soda to students at school.

4

The Categorical Imperative

I should never act except in such a way that I can also will that my maxim should become a universal law.

Immanuel Kant

Immanuel Kant developed his theory of ethics in response to David Hume's emotive theory of ethics. Kant's is a rational, not emotive, theory, in that a priori reasoning is the basis for his categorical principles. In *Grounding for the Metaphysics of Morals* (1785/1981), Kant states that "the ground of obligation here must therefore be sought not in the nature of man nor in the circumstances of the world in which man is placed, but must be sought a priori solely in the concepts of pure reason" (p. 12). Kant argued this point on the basis that logic cannot have any empirical part, that logic and universal laws of thought cannot be based solely on experience. His reasoning was that the laws of nature are based on what *does* happen, and the laws of ethical philosophy are those according to which everything *ought* to happen.

Kant states that if a law is to be ethically valid, it must carry with it absolute necessity and it must apply to all rational beings. Kant grants that rules based on empirical grounds can be called practical rules, but never ethical law. He states that ethical philosophy gives a priori laws to humans as rational beings, and even though humans are capable of pure practical reason, it is not so easy to make that idea effective in the day-to-day reality of life.

Kant asserts that morals "are liable to all kinds of corruption as long as the guide and supreme norm for correctly estimating them are missing. For in the case of what is to be morally good, that it conforms to moral law is not enough; it must also be done for the sake of the moral laws" (p. 3). Conformity to moral law is only contingent and uncertain because the non-moral ground may produce actions that conform to the law, but that also produce actions contrary to the law. From this point, Kant sets out to establish the supreme principle of morality.

Kant contends that the only thing that can be regarded as good, without qualification, is good will. In direct refutation of Hume, Kant explains, "A good will is good not because of what it effects or accomplishes . . . it is good only through its willing, i.e., it is good in itself" (p. 7).

Kant then develops the idea that existence of reason has a more worthy purpose than providing for happiness. "[I]ts true function must be to produce a will which is not merely good as a means to some further end, but is good in itself. To produce a will good in itself, reason was absolutely necessary, inasmuch as nature in distributing her capacities has everywhere gone to work in a purposive manner" (p. 9).

Kant here reveals his image of people as beings of nature with wills that are naturally good, who have the power of reason to guide the will toward good itself; he also contends that reason can lead people to things greater than mere happiness.

Kant presented three propositions of morality. The first one states "an action must be done from duty in order to have any moral worth" (p. 12). The second contends "an action done from duty has a moral worth independent of anything that is attained by that action, that the principle of volition itself has the moral worth" (p. 13). The third says that "duty is the necessity of an action done out of respect for the law" (p. 13).

Thus, the obligation exists to act in such a way that one would be willing to have one's own rules of practice made into universal principles that would apply equally to everyone. This is known as Kant's categorical imperative.

Kant has led us to a place where actions can be judged as ethically permissible, or impermissible, by their relation to duty. Regarding duty, he says, "Duty is the necessity of an action done out of respect for the law" (p. 14).

Kant identified four basic duties, two of which he identified as "perfect" duties, or those that permit no exception in the interest of one's inclination. His two examples of "perfect" duties are the duty to maintain one's life and the duty to keep promises made to others. The "imperfect" duties, or those that allow some discretion as to the allowance of one's inclination, are the duty to cultivate one's talents and the duty of beneficence to others.

Kant argued on behalf of the dignity and worth of all humans: "Rational beings are called persons inasmuch as their nature already marks them out as ends in themselves, which are thus objects of respect. Now, morality is the condition under which alone a rational being can be an end in himself, for only thereby can he be a legislating member in the kingdom of ends. . . . Thereby, he is free as regards all laws of nature, and he obeys only those laws which he gives to himself. Accordingly, his maxims can belong to a universal legislation to which he at the same time subjects himself" (pp. 35, 40–41).

Developing further the idea of autonomy of the will, Kant argued that the "autonomy of the will is the property that the will has of being a law unto itself" (p. 44), and that the principle of autonomy is basically to choose in such a way that "in the same volition the maxims of the choice are at the same time present as universal law" (p. 44). Concluding the argument on behalf of free will and autonomy, he argues, "What else, then, can freedom of the will be but autonomy, i.e., the property that the will has of being a law unto itself?" (p. 49).

KANT'S ETHICS AND THE CASE STUDIES

In examining the ethical issues that emerge from the upcoming case studies, it is important first to acknowledge that Kant would not be in favor of judging another person. He would expect people, as autonomous beings, to be much more interested in examining their own personal and professional behavior. In addition, to fully understand another's behavior, one would have to be able to know that person's maxims. The rule of universality as the sole means by which to assess the ethicality of decisions or actions leaves no room for interpretation and can appear simplistic.

The first ethical issue to confront is that of acting in regard to Kant's duty of being of benefit to others. Although it is impossible to get inside of other teachers' heads or fully understand their maxims, Kant's categorical imperative can be used to examine their behavior. As professional educators, teachers must carry out certain obligations, such as those spelled out in professional standards of behavior, including making the well-being of students the basis of all decisions and fulfilling professional responsibilities with integrity. Kant could argue that if teachers were to ignore students' needs in favor of their own, they would be treating their students as means toward their own ends, which is ethically impermissible.

Kant would maintain that in cases where civil law and moral law overlap, civil law supports moral law. He would also say that "duty is the necessity of an action done out of respect for the law" (p. 13). Therefore, teachers have the obligation to meet these duties of professional behavior. If teachers were to ignore civil law and these duties, they would be failing to keep the promises they made when they contracted to uphold the standards of their profession. Such actions would hurt the students and would hurt the credibility of other professionals in the organization.

If teachers are aware of any illegal practices taking place, they have the responsibility to report those violations to the proper authorities. By using the test of universality, such action is seen to be categorically imperative.

SUMMARY OF KANT'S ETHICS

Kant cleared the way out of the situational bog that characterizes Hume's theory. Where Hume argued that the ethicality of an action is based on its societally beneficial outcome, Kant said that if a law is to be ethically valid, it must be valid as a ground of obligation, it must carry with it absolute necessity, and it must apply equally to everyone.

Kant argued that the ground of obligation has to be sought neither in the nature of people nor in the circumstances of the world in which people are placed, but solely in the concepts of pure reason. In addition, he believed that virtue lies in the intent or maxim of an action, not in the action itself. Kant offers rational proof of a stable ethical foundation. He presents a way to build upon that foundation through categorical imperatives and the test of universality.

Kant believed in conscience. He pointed out that people are able to recognize whether their actions are motivated out of honest or dishonest intent, out of respect for ethical law, or out of self-interest. Kant's philosophy brings clarity and specificity into the process of decision making. According to Kant, if something is a rule for one person, it is a rule for everyone. There is no private morality. There are no private rules or exceptions that hold for some people and not others. So, with regard to the case studies, in asking "What if everyone were to do what I am about to do?", we can easily see whether or not that choice is the correct one—and be guided by that.

REFLECTION AND DISCUSSION QUESTIONS

1. Kant believed that reason, not emotion, should guide ethics. In comparing Hume and Kant, are you more inclined to agree with sentiment-based ethics or reason-based ethics?
2. Kant described two examples of "perfect" duties: the duty to maintain one's life and the duty to keep promises made to others. What do you think of the first perfect duty? Do people ever have the right to end their own life? Where are you on the second perfect duty? Do you keep promises made to others? How do you deal with promises you

wish you had not made? How do you deal with promises made to you by others that were not kept?

3. Kant described "imperfect" duties as those that allow some discretion as to the allowance of one's inclination, which are the duty to cultivate one's talents and the duty of beneficence to others. In what ways are you cultivating your talents? In what ways are you engaged in beneficence to others?

4. Kant could argue that if teachers were to ignore students' needs in favor of their own, they would be treating their students as means toward their own ends, which is ethically impermissible. What kinds of examples have you seen of educators ignoring students' needs in favor of their own needs? Do you think all of the behaviors in these examples are ethically impermissible?

5. Hume wouldn't necessarily condemn any particular action; the same action might be wrong in one situation and acceptable in another. Kant would say that the same action is either acceptable or not acceptable in all instances. What do you think of this difference in philosophies?

6. Kant articulated the "categorical imperative" that asserts that there is no such thing as private morality; all rules are for everyone. If people wonder about the ethicality of a personal decision or action, all they have to do is ask themselves: "What if everyone were to do what I am about to do? Would that be a good thing?" Give an example of using this idea, knowing it would *not* be a good thing if everyone did what you thinking about doing, but then think about going ahead and doing it anyway. What are the benefits? What are the problems?

7. Would Kant condone the act of driving a car above the speed limit to rush a loved one to the hospital emergency room?

8. Kant believed that people are able to recognize whether their actions are motivated out of honest or dishonest intent, out of respect for ethical law, or out of self-interest. What do you think? Are you always aware of the motives behind your actions? Do you think students are?

9. Describe some examples in which an action in a pre-K–12 environment is consistently wrong, no matter the situation.

10. Describe someone in your life who is like Kant.

11. Describe why you would, or would not, like to work for a principal who ascribed to Kant's ethics.

12. What do you think the strengths and weaknesses of Kant's ethics are in the pre-K–12 environment?

13. Compare and contrast Hume's ethics and Kant's ethics with regard to any issue in the school environment. For example:
    • Knowing a teacher who yells at students.
    • Tolerating an abusive principal in order to get a good evaluation.

- Giving extra time to a favorite at-risk student in timed, norm-referenced exams.
- Hearing teachers, during lunchtime in the staffroom, criticize students.
- Knowing a student who is emotionally abused at home.
- Knowing a colleague who, in the last year of work, is sloughing off.

5

The Greatest Good
for the Greatest Number

The idea of justice supposes two things: A rule of conduct and a sentiment
which sanctions the rule.

John Stuart Mill

In *Utilitarianism* (1861/1979), John Stuart Mill was looking for the middle
ground between David Hume and Immanuel Kant. He acknowledged that
there are two ways of looking at ethics: the inductive and the intuitive approaches. After discussing the merits and pitfalls of the two approaches,
Mill sided in favor of the inductive approach—he was, indeed, an empiricist and believed in using the data from reality and inductive reasoning to
arrive at principles of ethical behavior. According to a utilitarian view of
ethics, actions are right in proportion as they tend to promote happiness,
wrong if they tend to produce the reverse of happiness; pleasure and freedom from pain are the only things desirable as ends. Mill argued on behalf
of an empiricist approach, using inductive reasoning: "What is there to decide whether a particular pleasure is worth purchasing at the cost of a particular pain, except the feelings and judgment of the experienced? When,
therefore, those feelings and judgment declare the pleasures derived from
the higher faculties to be preferable in kind . . . to those of which the ani-
mal nature . . . is susceptible, they are entitled on this subject to the same
regard" (p. 11).

Mill's utilitarianism never sanctions self-benefit at the expense of society.
Mill explains, "The happiness which forms the utilitarian standard of what
is right in conduct is not the agent's own happiness but that of all concerned" (p. 16).

Mill's utilitarianism made the greatest break with other theories of ethics in arguing that when judging an action, a motive is of no value. However, Mill believed that the motive *does* have a great deal of value when looking at the worth of the person. Mill made another strong argument on behalf of an empirical approach to ethics in acknowledging that people have a vast background of experience and knowledge to draw upon in making ethical decisions.

The existence of a conscience, to Mill, was "a feeling in our own mind; a pain more or less intense" (p. 27), and the sense of conscience was the result of the way a person is taught. He contended that the ultimate sanction "of all morality is a subjective feeling" (p. 28).

Mill argued that freedom of choice holds enormous benefits for society, that one's own private interests count for no more than the interests of others, and that altruism is beneficial to society.

Mill defines justice as a sentiment by saying that justice is a utility: "We have seen that the two essential ingredients in the sentiment of justice are the desire to punish a person who has done harm and the knowledge or belief that there is some definite individual or individuals to whom harm has been done . . . the idea of justice supposes two things—a rule of conduct and a sentiment which sanctions the rule. The first must be supposed common to all mankind and intended for their good. The other (the sentiment) is a desire that punishment may be suffered by those who infringe the rule. [Justice is] a name for certain classes of moral rules which concern the essentials of human well-being more nearly, and are therefore of more absolute obligation, than any other rules for the guidance of life" (pp. 46–58).

Finally, Mill states that "justice remains the appropriate name for certain social utilities which are vastly more important, and therefore more absolute and imperative, than any others are as a class" (p. 63). Mill presented his theory of utilitarianism not as a theory endorsing expedient practices, but as a theory of ethical behavior devoted to the pursuit of happiness for all, one that appeals to the native sense of conscience. Mill's utilitarianism never sanctions self-benefit at the expense of society.

MILL'S ETHICS AND THE CASE STUDIES

Mill would argue that teachers should examine the entire scenario and take whatever action would produce the most desirable result for society. As professional educators facing ethically complex situations, teachers need to examine their primary responsibilities, which clearly fall on behalf of the students in their care.

According to Mill's philosophy, teachers' primary responsibilities are to provide students with the education and treatment that most effectively help them master the course content, lead them toward the most effective reasoning and decision making in their own lives, and prepare them to improve the condition of the world in which they live. By ignoring such responsibilities, teachers would be causing a great deal of pain for the students—and for society, which will soon be absorbing these students.

SUMMARY OF MILL'S ETHICS

Although Mill's theory of utilitarianism is often criticized for its perceived expediency, it can also be viewed as providing a variety of benefits. First, it is pragmatic and makes use of common frames of reference. Second, when applied as Mill intended, the theory insists that the greatest benefit of society, not one's own personal benefit, is of primary importance. Finally, Mill's description of justice allows more regard for the different and less precise applications of justice than mere civil law does.

The simplicity and pragmatic nature of Mill's theory, however, is offset by one great weakness: its relativity. The morality of an action, under Mill's theory, is determined by relative criteria. The greatest good must be quantified from a variety of possible outcomes and points of view before an action can be determined to be the appropriate one to take. This approach presents problems similar to those described in the assessment of Hume's theory, in that the morality of an action is based on its outcomes.

The "flexibility" of Mill's utilitarian theory of ethics is somewhat less problematic than is the "flexibility" of Hume's emotive theory of ethics, due to Mill's ideal of utilitarianism. Mill's theory of ethics is still problematic, however, because of its lack of firm criteria by which people can judge the ethicality of their actions.

REFLECTION AND DISCUSSION QUESTIONS

1. Mill believed in using the data from reality and inductive reasoning, not emotion or reason alone, to arrive at principles of ethical behavior. As a result, in Mill's utilitarian view of ethics, actions are right if they tend to promote happiness, wrong if they tend to produce the reverse of happiness. In other words, pleasure and freedom from pain are the only things desirable as ends. What do you think about this approach to ethical decision making?

2. Mill's utilitarian ethics do not support self-benefit at the expense of society. Mill says that the happiness that forms the utilitarian standard of what is right is not merely a person's own happiness, but the happiness of everybody concerned. So, clearly this moves beyond an "if it

feels good, do it" philosophy. Hume might say that it depends on the situation. Kant would say that teachers should not ignore students' needs in favor of their own, because doing so would be treating students as means toward their own ends, which is ethically impermissible. Mill says the prohibition against self-benefit would also make this wrong. Can you think of examples of educators' needs or interests over-riding students' needs or interests in the course of an ordinary school day?

3. Mill's says that when judging an action, a motive is of no value, but that the motive *does* have a great deal of value when looking at the worth of the person. How might this idea be useful in dealing with people's actions at school?

4. Mill would argue that in any given situation, teachers should examine the entire scenario and take whatever action would produce the most desirable result for society. Give some examples of how you think teachers, as a whole, do this well. Give some examples of how you think teachers, as a whole, fail miserably at doing this.

5. Hume wouldn't necessarily condemn any particular action; the same action might be wrong in one situation and acceptable in another. Kant would say that the same action is either acceptable or not acceptable in all instances. Mill would say that it depends on the outcomes and their benefit to the greater society. What do you think of these differences in philosophies?

6. How might these differences in philosophies look in regard to some deep societal issues, such as capital punishment, assisted suicide, abortion, or the legalization of marijuana?

7. At this point in your thinking and reflection, are you more inclined to resonate with rule-based ethics (Plato), sentiment-based ethics (Hume), reason-based ethics (Kant), or reality and inductive reasoning-based ethics (Mill)? Give some examples of, and reasons for, your thinking.

8. Describe some examples in which an action in a pre-K–12 environment might or might not be permissible, depending on the outcome.

9. Describe someone in your life who is like Mill.

10. Describe why you would, or would not, like to work for a principal who ascribes to Mill's utilitarian ethics.

11. What are the strengths and weaknesses of Mill's ethics in the school environment?

12. You see that considering what is of the greatest good for society as a basis for ethical decision making amplifies the complexity of what teachers do. To explore this complexity, compare and contrast Plato's, Hume's, Kant's, and Mill's ethics with regard to any issue in the school environment. For example:

- Eliminating recess to provide more instructional time.
- Eliminating art, music, and/or physical education to provide more time for reading and math.
- Glossing over science because it is more important to teach reading and math.
- Using class time to review and practice for norm-referenced tests.
- Pretending to get along with an abusive principal in order to get a good evaluation, in order to get a job as a principal, in order to make changes you believe need to be made in schools.
- Putting all the difficult boys in one class because "that teacher can handle them."
- Having the whole school use an additional week of instructional time to prepare, review, and practice for norm-referenced exams.
- Knowing of a romantic relationship between a teacher and a principal.
- Cheating on a test in order to pass a class, in order to graduate, in order to get out into the real world and do good work for others.
- Allocating more money in technology than in hiring school counselors.

6

The Heroic Ideal and Self-Interest

The moral absolute should be: If and when, in any dispute, one side initiates the use of physical force, that side is wrong.

Ayn Rand

Objectivism, the name Ayn Rand gave to the philosophical system she developed and refined, is an integrated system of thought that attempts to define the principles by which we must think and act if we are to live our lives as proper human beings. Objectivism is a rational philosophy by which, according to Rand, people can attain the best in human achievement. According to Rand: "Man must choose his actions, values, and goals by the standard of that which is proper to man in order to achieve, maintain, fulfill, and enjoy that ultimate value, that end in itself, which is his own life" (1961).

The central concept of objectivism is man as a heroic being with his own happiness as the purpose for his existence, productive achievement as his greatest activity, and reason as his only absolute. Contained within Rand's philosophy of Objectivism are the four interlocking dynamics of metaphysics, epistemology, politics, and ethics.

Metaphysics is a term for our understanding of the universe. In Objectivist philosophy, existence does not need to be explained. Existence exists. We can ask why something exists, but not why existence exists. It just does. Rand would say that if we were to ask why existence exists, or what created the universe, we would then have to ask why *that* exists or who created *that*. So, Objectivism starts with the notion that existence does not need to be explained, that existence exists. We perceive our reality through our senses, and logic begins with the evidence provided by our senses. The opposite of this *objective* reality is *subjective* reality, a reality dependent upon the opinions and wishes of individuals. In other words, we can perceive reality, but we cannot create it. Facts are facts and reality is an objective absolute. In the simplest of terms, A equals A.

Epistemology is a term that describes our means of acquiring knowledge. According to Rand's Objectivist philosophy, *reason* is our only way of attaining knowledge, and the ability to form concepts is the main function of the faculty of reason. We are rational animals and our highest virtue is the ability to think. As rational animals, there can be no tolerance for subjectivism in which knowledge is merely opinion. Objectivism does not condone skepticism because skepticism promotes the idea that no one can really be certain of anything. Objectivism also rejects mysticism on the grounds that if one can only know something through a supernatural dimension, logic or reason cannot be present. Reason is our basic means of survival and the only way to determine our actions.

Politics are the standards by which people choose their goals and values in regards to society. The political basis of Objectivism is that individual rights are paramount, and the only just government is one that limits itself in protecting individual rights and property. A government that forces financial contributions, forbids the free exchange of goods, redistributes income, and provides central services, such as education and health care, is, through an Objectivist philosophy, considered to be both unjust and morally invalid. Capitalism, or, more precisely, laissez-faire capitalism, is at the heart of the Objectivist political view of social structure, in which people are viewed as producers and traders, voluntarily exchanging goods and services and ideas for mutual benefit. Objectivism is opposed to any kind of social engineering or any attempts to legislate behavior. Consequently, no person should obtain something from someone else by force, duress, or someone else's perceptions of obligation. In the Objectivist philosophy, people have the right to live by their own minds, in their own way, and for their own sake.

To understand ethics, one must understand what values are and why we need them. Accordingly, Rand asks, "Why does man need a code of values?" (1961, p. 14). She questions what it is in our existence that makes necessary the concept of values. Rand defines values as "something that one acts to gain and/or to keep" (p. 16). For rational beings, values lead to choices. Rand condemns the ethical choices that have been made in history as the result of emotions, social edicts, and mysticism. Almost without exception, "moralists have regarded ethics as the province of whims, that is, of the irrational" (p. 14).

Mysticism and religion have based their morality on some higher standard of good that has been handed down through the ages. Modern philosophies explain their standard of value as what is good for society. Objectivism views these standards as types of irrational thinking that have led to society's deciding to do whatever it chooses to do merely because it chooses to do it. Insofar as society is made up of large numbers of people, then every individual in that number is subject to the values of others—which, in the Objectivist philosophy, is wrong.

The three cardinal values of Objectivist ethics, the three values that together are the means and the realization of one's ultimate value, one's own life, are: reason, purpose, self-esteem, with their three corresponding virtues of rationality, productiveness, pride (Rand, 1961, p. 27). Objectivism is clear in its rejection of altruism. Acting solely for the good of another requires us to sacrifice our own values. Acting according to the values of another is considered to be highly immoral and leads to the destruction of self. This prohibition against acting for the good of others, however, does not preclude one's chosen obligations. One's moral responsibility is to one's self, one's values, one's chosen obligations.

OBJECTIVISM AND THE CASE STUDIES

One of the more difficult aspects of Objectivism is the relegation of feelings and emotions to the realm of the irrational. Objectivism would hold that unless one can reason through logic that feelings are rational, the feelings must be dismissed as a basis for ethical decision making. Acting on impulse or whim will not generally result in lasting happiness. Happiness results only when one achieves the values that are derived from using one's reason. Teachers, and other people in the people-helping professions, tend to be emotive and responsive to other people's emotional needs, sometimes at the expense of their own well-being.

Some of the upcoming case studies highlight the conflict between self-interest and the interests of others, especially students. Superficially, living for one's self-interest might appear to be synonymous with living purely for one's pleasure. Rand identifies the fallacy inherent in seeing Objectivism as hedonism. If one lives with the goal of only achieving gratification of one's desires, conflict will necessarily arise. One person's desires will necessitate the sacrifice of another's desires, which will result in destruction of one or the other's self. That would not be a rational code of ethics that required the obliteration of one person's happiness over another's because it would result in neither one succeeding. Living for one's self-interest does not mean sacrificing others. Nor does living for one's self-interest mean sacrificing for others—unless doing so is a value for that person. People tend to gravitate toward teaching because they value helping others, yet conflicts in whose interests come first arise continually.

With laissez-faire capitalism at the heart of the objectivist view of society, in which people are viewed as producers and traders, voluntarily exchanging goods and services and ideas for mutual benefit, a tremendous array of issues emerge with regard to the public school system. Because Objectivism is opposed to social engineering, the legislation of behavior, the use of duress, force, or other's perceptions or requirements of obligation, and because Objectivism would oppose the idea of people being required to pay for services they either do not want or that they can provide for themselves, the whole notion of a public school system would seem to be under attack.

Objectivism emphasizes reason, individual rights, enlightened self-interest, political and economic freedom, and, most importantly, a heroic vision of life's possibilities. Objectivism encourages us to explore our own power and potential, and states that life is about achievement and joy. Some of the case studies highlight an array of issues that arise when one's heroic ideal is in conflict with that of another—often a superior, a senior colleague, or a student's parent. Objectivism would insist that we use reason, logic, knowledge, and skill, not ideology, position, favoritism, or seniority, to decide upon a course of action.

SUMMARY OF OBJECTIVIST ETHICS

Rand was not a trained philosopher. Rand chose to present her theories through stage plays, screenplays, and novels rather than through scholarly journals. As a result, academics have often refused to give Objectivism much credit. The positions Rand presented, particularly on self-interest and capitalism, were not widely held beliefs in the 1940s and 1950s, which is when she did most of her work, and they presented a radical departure from the conventional thinking of the time. An enduring problem has been the difference between what she terms *rational self-interest* and the negative connotations inherent in *selfishness*. In addressing this, Rand said: "I would step in the way of a bullet if it were aimed at my husband. It is not self-sacrifice to die protecting that which you value: If the value is great enough, you do not care to exist without it. This applies to any alleged sacrifice for those one loves" (Rand, 1961, p. 49).

The most damning criticism against Objectivism, however, has to do with the morally uncompromising position that the only acceptable errors are errors of knowledge, and that errors of morality are unforgivable. Rand said: "Learn to distinguish between errors of knowledge and breaches of morality. An error of knowledge is not a moral flaw, providing you are willing to correct it. But a breach of morality is the conscious choice of an action you know to be evil. Make every allowance for errors of knowledge; do not forgive or accept any breach of morality" (Rand, 1957, p. 974).

Acquiring knowledge is not a passive activity. Rather, it requires the act of thinking. Reason is the faculty that sets us apart from other living organisms, and we must take an active role in developing our ability to reason. In order to go through the process of thinking, we must use the laws of logic. Logic and reason are the basic elements of the Objectivist philosophy. Knowledge is the key to survival. Choosing not to think will result in, and has resulted in, negative consequences. Because we do not act automatically in ways that satisfy our natural needs, we must exercise free choice. "Man is the only living species that has the power to act as his own destroyer, and that is the way he has acted through most of his history" (Rand, 1961, p. 25).

Objectivism presents challenges to our current assumptions of how to live a good life. One of its major contributions resonates with an array of philosophers: People are rational beings who can, and should, use reason to live their lives according to their own heroic ideals.

REFLECTION AND DISCUSSION QUESTIONS

1. How is Objectivism's "enlightened self-interest" similar to, and different from, the "self-interest" of David Hume?
2. How is Objectivism's "enlightened self-interest" similar to, and different from, the "self-interest" of John Stuart Mill?
3. What do you see as the differences between self-interest and selfishness?
4. Rand says to "Make every allowance for errors of knowledge; do not forgive or accept any breach of morality" (Rand, 1957, p. 974). What are your thoughts about this? Have you ever been forgiven for a breach of morality? If so, did being forgiven serve you well?
5. What is your heroic ideal for your own life?
6. Rand says, "If the value is great enough, you do not care to exist without it. This applies to any alleged sacrifice for those one loves" (Rand, 1961, p. 49). Does your love for teaching fall into this category and excuse you from Rand's criticism of self-sacrifice?
7. How might the use of reason, logic, knowledge, and skill, rather than ideology, position, favoritism, or seniority, affect some of the decisions we make in the school environment?
8. Is your own life, as an end in itself, your ultimate value?
9. What aspects of Objectivism resonate with you?
10. What aspects of Objectivism do you find objectionable?
11. Describe someone in your life who is like Rand.
12. Describe why you would, or would not, like to work for a principal who ascribed to Objectivist ethics.

13. What are the strengths and weaknesses of Objectivist ethics in the school environment?

14. The Objectivist prohibition against altruism, against acting for the good of others, does not preclude one's chosen obligations. How would Rand, how will you, identify the boundaries between a teacher's chosen obligation of meeting students' needs and the host of other student-related obligations society expects of teachers?

15. How might Objectivist ethics regard some deep societal issues, such as private-pay versus publicly supported health care systems, capital punishment, assisted suicide, abortion, the legalization of marijuana, or stem cell research?

16. Compare and contrast Plato's, Hume's, Kant's, Mill's, and Objectivist ethics with regard to any issue in the school environment. For example:

    • A school board's decision to eliminate art, music, and/or physical education classes in order to provide more time for reading and math.

    • A teacher's decision to gloss over science because reading is more important.

    • A teacher's pretending to get along with an abusive principal in order to get a good evaluation, in order to get a job as a principal, in order to make changes that he or she believes need to be made in schools.

    • A principal and a teacher in the same building engaging in a romantic relationship.

    • A teacher and an 18-year-old senior engaging in a romantic relationship.

    • A school board's decision to require that students wear uniforms.

    • A school board's decision to require abstinence-based sex education.

    • A teacher's decision to teach yoga for its calming effects in her third grade class.

    • A teacher sloughing off in his or her last year of teaching.

    • A school board's decision to invest more funding in technology than in hiring school counselors.

7

Absolute Truth and Nonviolence

Morality is the basis of things, and truth is the substance of all morality.

Gandhi

Mohandas Gandhi left a powerful impact on the world's history. His personal way of life was as much an influence on making societal and political changes as his actions.

Gandhi demonstrated that personal reflection was a practical endeavor for a political leader. Although action was his domain, his first activity of the day was to spend at least an hour in prayer and meditation (Nair, 1997).

Gandhi's life was a creative ongoing experiment that remained true to his beliefs while still being flexible enough to respond to world events. Gandhi believed that "all religions were manifestation of the Truth and that people of different faiths should and could live in peace and harmony" (Nair, 1997, p. 5). Gandhi had a fundamental belief in nonviolence. Throughout his life, he believed that action required personal service to others.

Gandhi's own life was the best practical example of his beliefs and his ethics. In an age when the place of the individual was being challenged and the specter of total mass-control was raised on every hand, Gandhi had insisted that no power on earth could make a man do a thing against his will. (Bondurant, 1965)

Born in 1869, Gandhi's early years in Porbandar, India, were traditional Hindi-Indian. He was 13 years old when he married Kasturbai. Even though Kasturbai was to have a long and supportive role in Gandhi's work, later in his life Gandhi questioned the validity of childhood marriages. His education was also traditional, until he decided he wanted to study law in England in 1888. Exposure to English society prompted him to question his traditions of faith and diet. It also put him in contact with a wide circle of friends with a wide variety of ideas.

Upon his return to India, he found that there was no role or position for him to fill, so he accepted an opportunity to work as a lawyer for a firm of Porbandar Moslems in South Africa. There, he was exposed to racial injustice—which had a profound influence on his life. On his way to Pretoria by train and although he possessed a first-class ticket, the officials threw him off the train because of his color. "I began to think of my duty. Should I fight for my rights or go back to India. It would be cowardice to run back to India without fulfilling my obligation" (Gandhi, 1958/1999, p. 114). This event would develop the seeds for what we have come to know as Gandhi's *passive resistance*. Gandhi called this type of resistance *satyagraha*, which means "holding on to the truth," and he called his method *ahimsa*, meaning "nonviolence; the practice of love."

During his years in Africa, Gandhi worked to support the expatriate Indian community and "organize his convictions into a form others would understand and respond to" (Kytle, 1982, p. 64). At the age of 46, Gandhi returned to India, where "his reputation as the leader of an effective movement against British rule in South Africa had traveled ahead of him. Within three years, he had made his way into the inner circle of India's embryonic national movement" (Juergensmeyer, 1986, p. 137).

For the first year and a half back in India, Gandhi followed the advice of G. K. Gokhale, a leader in the Indian nationalism movement, who said he should get to know the people and their grievances by traveling "with his ears open and his mouth shut" (Kytle, 1982, p. 104). This period of travel and observation ended when Gandhi gave a speech at the Hindu University Central College that included native princes and Indian civil servants who catered to British rule. Gandhi explained that self-government would require two foci: commitment to civil disobedience and, concurrently, service to the poor. He explained that this path to self-government would occur only when Indian leaders started to meet the needs of the villagers rather than those of the British.

From 1916 on, Gandhi involved himself in major facets of political life in India. He organized national strikes and huge marches. He gave speeches and wrote. He fasted. All of his actions on behalf of the poor and the move toward self-government were anchored in, and demonstrated by, his beliefs of absolute truth, nonviolence, and action by way of service to the poor. "If we act justly, India will be free sooner. You will see, too, that if we shun every Englishman as an enemy, Home Rule will be delayed. But if we are just to them, we shall receive their support" (Fisher, 1954, p. 52).

Gandhi also spent a great deal of time examining traditional beliefs and behaviors within the social fabric of Indian life. For example, he refused to accept the beliefs and practices that created and shunned one group of Indians, the so-called Untouchables, from interacting with the rest of the population.

On January 30, 1948, a member of a radical Hindu sect bowed to Gandhi and then assassinated him. Gandhi was killed, but his way of life reshaped history and enriched the lives of millions of people around the world. When Gandhi died, he "was what he had always been: a private citizen without wealth, property, title, official position, academic distinction, or scientific achievement" (Fisher, 1954, p. 7). The world knew that when Gandhi was killed, "the conscience of mankind had been left without a spokesman. Humanity was impoverished because a poor man had died" (p. 7).

GANDHI'S ETHICAL PRINCIPLES

Gandhi's most prevailing principles were his commitment to absolute truth and nonviolence. His first moral and ethical principle, truth, or *satyagraha*, crossed all barriers. Being a religious man did not limit his appeal because his definition of truth was boundless: "To me, God is Truth and Love. God is ethics and morality. God is fearlessness. God is the source of Light and Life, and yet He is above and beyond all these. God is conscience. He is even the atheism of the atheist. He transcends speech and reason. He is all things to all men" (Gandhi, 1958/1999, p. 53).

Gandhi's second moral and ethical principle, nonviolence, or *ahimsa*, was guided by the positive love for humanity and the complete abstention from exploitation in any form. Gandhi knew that the possibility of perfect nonviolence was impossible because a physical body must inhabit space, but that "we have to endeavour every moment of our lives" (p. 83).

It is apparent that the reason Gandhi never disliked his opponents was because he believed that part of nonviolence requires the love for all. "It is not nonviolence if we merely love those that love us. It is nonviolence only when we love those that hate us" (p. 78). Therefore, it was difficult for his opponents to refuse to negotiate with him or, at the very least, respect him, because he respected them. As Gandhi explained it, "Let us honour our opponents for the same honesty of purpose and patriotic motives that we claim for ourselves" (p. 157).

Through his commitment to truth and nonviolence, Gandhi developed principles for character and leadership: "A leader is useless when he acts against the prompting of his own conscience, surrounded, as he must be, by people holding all kinds of views. He will drift like an anchorless ship if he has not the inner voice to hold him firm and guide him" (p. 132).

Gandhi believed that the follower and the leader co-existed without distinction. There could not be a leader unless there were people who wished to follow. Yet, each leader had to be guided by his or her commitment to truth—which didn't necessarily necessitate consistency of action. "I am not at all concerned with appearing to be consistent. In my pursuit after Truth, I have discarded many ideas and learnt many new things" (Gandhi, 1999, p. 155).

Nair (1997) presents a layered overview of how Gandhi's commitments to truth and nonviolence might look as principles for leadership. First is a single standard of conduct for both public and private life. Second is truthful service to others. When people are committed to truth and service, and not to power and popularity, unpleasant truths can be told. The third principle is that all decisions and actions must be filtered through truth, nonviolence, and the universal code—which is to treat others as ourselves.

GANDHI'S ETHICS AND THE CASE STUDIES

Some of the upcoming case studies involve workplace-specific examples of violence: bullying, conspiring against colleagues, and betraying confidences. Clearly, Gandhi would argue that truth and nonviolence should always be upheld.

As professional educators facing ethically complex situations, teachers need to examine whether there is a proper time or role for secrets and whether there are times that the truth simply cannot be told.

Teachers' primary responsibilities are to help students grow academically and emotionally. Yet, in the day-to-day operation of the school and the classroom, students' needs are sometimes the last things that get considered. Ignoring students' academic and emotional needs might be seen by Gandhi as a form of violence, as might outdated curriculum, other teaching materials, and location-specific resources that put some children at a disadvantage.

SUMMARY OF GANDHI'S ETHICS

A summary of Gandhi's ethics is simple and straightforward: absolute truth, nonviolence, and a commitment to action on behalf of the underserved.

REFLECTION AND DISCUSSION QUESTIONS

1. The basis of Gandhi's thought is that truth and nonviolence are the fundamental principles from which all rules of ethics are derived. Can you use truth and nonviolence as a guiding principle in your decision making?

2. Gandhi said that perfect nonviolence is not attainable because we are physical beings that occupy space. How do you interpret this?
3. If we were to use absolute truth and nonviolence as guiding principles in our decision making, how would this affect the numbers of students and teachers who are not happy in our current school system?
4. How might the concept of *treating others as we wish to be treated* as a guiding principle in your decision making create problems for people in your daily actions?
5. Describe some examples of school-based situations that might present a conflict if you were to follow the principles of absolute truth and nonviolence with students, colleagues, administrators, and parents.
6. How do you define the boundary between being of service to others and the daily reality of taking care of yourself, your family, and your career?
7. How might Gandhi's ethics treat some deep societal issues, such as capital punishment, suicide, assisted suicide, abortion, legalization of marijuana, stem cell research, or funding military weaponry for other countries?
8. At this point in your thinking and reflection, are you more inclined to resonate with rule-based ethics (Plato), sentiment-based ethics (Hume), reason-based ethics (Kant), reality and inductive reasoning-based ethics (Mill), Objectivism (Rand), or truth and nonviolence-based ethics (Gandhi)? Give some examples of, and reasons for, your thinking.
9. Describe someone in your life who acts in a Gandhi-like manner.
10. Describe why you would, or would not, like to work for a principal who ascribed to Gandhi's truth and nonviolence-based ethics.
11. What are the strengths and weaknesses of Gandhi's approach to ethical decision making in the school environment? How might this approach work better, or worse, in some settings than in others?
12. What are the similarities and differences between Objectivism's self-interest and individualism and Gandhi's duty to be of service to others?
13. What kinds of things do we simply *have* to keep secret?
14. Are there ways we use secrecy to exclude people (students, teachers, or parents) who don't fit in?
15. Are there ways in which the evaluation of performance, of either students or teachers in the K–12 system, leads to untruthful practices?
16. "A commitment to the truth provides the best defense against two of the most common errors in strategic decision making: rush to judgment and group-think" (Nair, 1997, p. 126). What are some examples from your own experience?
17. Is it realistic to set a goal for zero defects in truth in the K–12 environment?

18. Can you describe a situation in which leaders take an advocacy position and neglect facts that do not support their position?
19. What are some things Rand and Gandhi would absolutely agree on?
20. What are some things Rand and Gandhi would absolutely disagree on?
21. Using truth, nonviolence, and action in service to others as a basis for ethical decision making presents a new perspective for examining the array of decisions educators make every day, and the actions they take, with students, colleagues, administrators, parents, committees, the community, their families, and themselves. To more fully explore this complexity, examine Gandhi's ethics with regard to any issue in the school environment. For example:
    - Poverty- and race-based differences in the public school system.
    - Teachers' preparation for the sociocultural aspects of teaching.
    - A teacher hiring a student to work in his private business.
    - A principal directing a new teacher to teach outside of his or her skill area.
    - A district, school, or teacher eliminating recess to provide more instructional time.
    - A district eliminating art, music, or physical education to create more time for reading and math.
    - A teacher providing more than the allowed amount of recess time.
    - A teacher, school, or district using class time to review for norm-referenced tests.
    - A teacher complaining to a superintendent about a difficult principal, rather that speaking directly with the principal.
    - A teacher giving girls different consequences for bad behavior than he or she gives the boys.
    - A teacher's decision to teach yoga for its calming effects in her third grade class.
    - Two teachers criticizing another teacher behind her back.
    - A school district implementing a non-research-based, abstinence-only sex education program.

8

Respect for Persons

> The idea of the individual person as one of supreme worth is fundamental to the ethical, political, and religious ideals of our society.
>
> Downie and Telfer

In *Respect for Persons* (1969), R. S. Downie and Elizabeth Telfer present a theory of ethics that synthesizes the key elements of the four theories discussed so far. Their theory can be summed up as follows: Respect for persons is the single fundamental principle from which all rules of ethics are derived.

Downie and Telfer begin with the notion that "the idea of the individual person as one of supreme worth is fundamental to the ethical, political, and religious ideals of our society" (p. 9). They refer to Kant's and Mill's philosophical works as examples in which this idea is given a central role. Downie and Telfer hold that people are intrinsically valuable in and of themselves. They contend that what is worthy of respect in a person is the ability to exercise rational will in self-determination and rule following.

Downie and Telfer deal with Mill's utilitarianism by saying that "it is unintelligible to suppose that happiness matters without supposing that the people whose happiness is in question matter" (p. 39). They believe that the "principle of liberty may conflict with the positive aspects of utility. These positive aspects stress the importance of achieving the maximum satisfaction of interests, and for this to be possible, some degree of social cooperation is necessary" (p. 57). This position requires an understanding of liberty that has both a positive and a negative side, with the negative side consisting of refraining from interference in people's pursuits of their aims and in not causing them pain or distress.

Downie and Telfer state that people have basic duties to themselves to develop their human nature, called *duties of private morality*, and contend that in developing natural talents, a person is fulfilling the requirements of private morality. They form a certain symmetry between respect for others and self-respect by arguing that self-respect is to private morality what respect for others is to public morality. This argument is based on two premises: first, that if people take respect for others to be equivalent to respect for themselves, the sense of *self* in both cases is the same; and second, that the sense of *respect* is the same in both cases. Downie and Telfer hold that public morality and private morality are not two moralities, "but two aspects of a single fundamental moral principle" (p. 84).

DOWNIE AND TELFER'S ETHICS AND THE CASE STUDIES

Respect for persons as the ultimate principle of morality makes the proper course of action for teachers clear. Downie and Telfer would argue that moral rules exist and provide safe guidance for the array of ethically complex situations schoolteachers face. These ethical rules exist because people have learned by experience that certain types of action are liable to have consequences that are either good or bad. Is it right for a teacher to do anything that harms a student or another teacher? No. Would it be right for a teacher to ignore such an event? No. Are teachers obligated to follow the legally prescribed actions if such behavior occurs? Yes, out of respect for others and for themselves.

SUMMARY OF DOWNIE AND TELFER'S ETHICS

Downie and Telfer have successfully synthesized a theory of ethics based on Plato, Hume, Kant, and Mill. They have incorporated the concern for reason that exemplifies the idealistic and rationalistic theories of Plato and Kant. They have taken into account the feelings critical to the emotive theory of Hume. They have paid attention to the virtue ethics of Plato and Hume, and have retained the principles of Kant's and Mill's theories. The strength of Downie and Telfer's theory of ethics is not its originality, but the skillful interweaving of its underlying principles.

The single greatest conflict in Downie and Telfer's theory is that because both duty to self and duty to others are binding, one must sometimes choose between the two. They answer this problem to a degree in their discussion of self-referring morality. Basically, they contend that if morality is to be self-referring, it involves a kind of respect, which means maintaining autonomy or self-control. This approach seems to move in the opposite direction from Hume's theory, in which exists the problem of not being able to look far enough into the future to assess the consequences of an action. With Downie and Telfer's theory, people can look to the here and now for evidence of self-control, and to respect for others as guides for ethical decision making.

SUMMARY OF ETHICAL PERSPECTIVES

The concepts of justice, sentiment, reason, benefit, and respect have been explored and described for centuries. These concepts were analyzed in the preceding section and reveal a broad range of ethical principles. They form a continuum of concerns people must face in making difficult decisions.

The intent of the last seven chapters is to articulate a wide range of ethical bases and to show how different concerns and conceptualizations of justice can play out differently with regard to ethically complex situations. Different aspects of ethical decision-making theories were presented in order to interpret how individuals deal with issues of ethical compromise and the decisions they make. These chapters show that not all ethical bases are the same, and that people can use a variety of ethical theories in order to make difficult decisions.

REFLECTION AND DISCUSSION QUESTIONS

1. The basis for Downie and Telfer's theory is that *respect for persons* is the single fundamental principle from which all rules of ethics are derived. What do you think about this approach to ethical decision making? Do you feel respect from the people in your personal and professional life? Can you use *respect for persons* as a guiding principle in your decision making?

2. Can you use the idea of the individual as one of supreme worth being fundamental to the ethical, political, and religious ideals of our society as a guiding principle in working with students and colleagues in the school environment?

3. In referring to Mill's utilitarianism, Downie and Telfer say, "It is unintelligible to suppose that happiness matters without supposing that the people whose happiness is in question matter" (1969, p. 39). What do you think of this? If we were to use this as a guiding principle in our decision making, how would we talk about and deal with the numbers of students and teachers who are not happy in our current school system?

4. Much like Kant, Downie and Telfer state that people have basic duties to themselves to develop their human nature, which they call *duties of private morality*, and they contend that in developing natural talents, a person is fulfilling the requirements of private morality. What natural talents are you developing? How has your awareness of, or interest in, your natural talents changed over the years? Are there people or dynamics in your life that are keeping you from developing your natural talents?

5. Downie and Telfer say that self-respect is to private morality what respect for others is to public morality. Whether or not you consciously use *respect for persons* as a guiding principle in your decision making, how does your respect for others show up in your daily actions?

6. The single greatest conflict in Downie and Telfer's approach to ethical decision making is that because both duty to self and duty to others are binding, one must sometimes choose between the two. Teachers are faced with this kind of conflict every day. Describe some examples of school-based situations that might present a conflict between your duty to self and your duty to others, such as students, colleagues, administrators, and parents.

7. Downie and Telfer suggest that the way to manage such conflicts between duty to self and duty to others is by maintaining autonomy or self-control. What kinds of boundaries do you think are important for teachers to establish that would help them manage conflicts between duty to self and duty to others?

8. How do you describe the difference between self-interest and duty to self?

9. Mill would argue that in any given situation, teachers should examine the entire scenario and take whatever action would produce the most desirable result for society. Downie and Telfer's approach suggests that teachers might take whatever action would be the most respectful for an individual. How might these two approaches produce conflict in schools? How might these two approaches be harmonized in a school-based situation?

10. At this point in your thinking and reflection, are you more inclined to resonate with rule-based ethics (Plato), sentiment-based ethics (Hume), reason-based ethics (Kant), reality and inductive reasoning-based ethics (Mill), truth and nonviolence-based ethics (Gandhi), Objectivism (Rand), or respect-based ethics (Downie and Telfer)? Give some examples of, and reasons for, your thinking.

11. How might an ethics of respect for persons regard some deep societal issues, such as suicide, assisted suicide, private-pay versus publicly supported health care systems, capital punishment, abortion, legalization of marijuana, stem cell research, funding military weaponry

for other countries, or governmental support/requirement/avoidance of reductions in greenhouse gas emissions?

12. Describe someone in your life who acts in a Downie and Telfer-like manner.
13. Describe why you would, or would not, like to work for a principal who ascribed to Downie and Telfer's respect for persons-based ethics.
14. What are the strengths and weaknesses of Downie and Telfer's approach to ethical decision making in the school environment? How might this approach work better, or worse, in some settings than in others?
15. What are the similarities and differences between Objectivism's self-interest and Downie and Telfer's duty to self?
16. In what ways do you respect the intrinsic good in every individual?
17. How might it look to include moral criteria in evaluating decisions and actions?
18. Are there ways in which we encourage violence to persons in the workplace?
19. Do teachers ever put their interests above the public good? If so, is that a bad thing?
20. How does it feel to not live up to an ideal?
21. What are some of the forces that lead us astray from living up to the ideal?
22. Is "Jiminy Cricket" still alive?
23. "Many of us can look back at situations and ask, 'Why didn't somebody say something?'" (Nair, 1997, p. 136). What are some examples of this from your own experience?
24. Have you ever exercised your moral courage to do what you know is right and faced adversity as a result?
25. Using respect for persons as a basis for ethical decision making presents a new perspective for examining the array of decisions educators make every day, and the actions they take, with students, colleagues, administrators, parents, committees, the community, their families, and themselves. To more fully explore this complexity, compare and contrast Plato's, Hume's, Kant's, Mill's, Gandhi's, Rand's, and Downie and Telfer's ethics with regard to any issue in the school environment. For example:
    - A romantic relationship between a teacher and principal.
    - A budding romance between an 18-year-old student and a 22-year-old teacher.
    - A principal whose child is a student in your classroom.
    - A teacher hiring a student to work in his private business.
    - A principal hiring a teacher more for fitting into the community than for expertise.

- A principal directing a new teacher to teach outside of his or her skill area.
- A district, school, or teacher eliminating recess to provide more instructional time.
- A district eliminating art, music, or physical education to create more time for reading and math.
- A teacher glossing over science in order to teach reading and math.
- A teacher, school, or district using class time to review for norm-referenced tests.
- A teacher pretending to get along with a difficult administrator in order to get a good evaluation, in order to get a job as a principal, in order to make changes that he or she believes need to be made in schools.
- A teacher complaining to a superintendent about a difficult principal, rather that speaking directly with the principal.
- A principal or a committee putting all the difficult boys in one class because "that teacher can handle them."
- A superintendent going against an interview committee's recommendation for the hiring of a new principal.
- A school board re-instituting an academic achievement-based student retention policy.
- A school board refusing to consider adding wellness days, in addition to sick days, to their collective agreements with teachers.

9

Emotions, Intellect, Stress, and Ethics: A Family Systems Approach

Anyone can become angry—that is easy. But to be angry with the right person, to the right degree, at the right time, for the right purpose, and in the right way, this is not easy.

Aristotle

It is impossible for there to be more than a relative separation between emotional and intellectual functioning, but those whose intellectual functioning can retain relative autonomy in periods of stress are more flexible, more adaptable, and more independent of the emotionality about them. They cope better with life stresses, their life courses are more orderly and successful, and they are remarkably free of human problems.

Murray Bowen

The purpose of this chapter is to explain this book's approach to examining and dealing with ethically complex situations, in part, by also examining our thoughts, feelings, and actions. Thoughts and feelings are human beings' basic emotional and intellectual navigation systems; they are the two systems we use to engage in any kind of interaction. Thoughts and feelings, and the ways in which we manage them, are the major dynamics of Family Systems Theory. Accordingly, the decision to approach the following case studies about ethically complex situations in schools is guided by the theoretical perspective of family systems theory.

FAMILY SYSTEMS THEORY

Murray Bowen, M.D., developed family systems theory in the 1950s and 1960s. The theory was more thoroughly articulated throughout the 1970s and 1980s by Murray Bowen and Michael Kerr, M.D. The application of family systems theory to our work with complex ethical situations in schools is appropriate for at least three reasons. Family systems theory views the family as an emotional unit, not just as a collection of individuals. Family systems theory identifies several important variables that influence physical, emotional, and social problems in the family—or, in our case, schools—as an emotional unit. Finally, family systems theory demonstrates that the interrelationship of these variables can be understood with *systems* thinking; that is, rather than seeing physical, emotional, and social problems as *cause and effect* dynamics, they can more accurately be seen as part of a *relationship* process.

Although Bowen (1978) created the family systems model for family therapy, it has been extended beyond what we define as a family, to include other social groupings. The concept of emotional process has been applied to larger social systems, such as ethnic, national, and cultural groupings by Friedman (1985) and Cameron (2001). These larger groupings are subject to the same laws governing the family system: increased anxiety will decrease the functional level of individuals and groups. Titelman (1988) says, "The emotional viability of larger groups ultimately rests on the level of differentiation of the individuals within that group and their capacity and willingness to deal with anxiety" (p. 13).

Just as families are governed by their own emotional systems, so, too, are larger social systems. With regard to schools, Cameron (2001) suggests a group's emotional system is particularly influential in a time of heightened anxiety. "The emotional system influences all of the system's actions—from forming social relationships to responding to trauma" (p. 38). According to Kerr and Bowen (1988), "every family emotional system generates certain functions . . . when one individual performs certain functions, other individuals will not perform them" (p. 315).

DIFFERENTIATION OF SELF

Bowen suggests that differentiation, which is "the degree to which people are able to distinguish between the feeling process and the intellectual process" (1978, p. 88), is key to being a successful family member. For our purposes, this differentiation of self, this ability to distinguish between the feeling process and the intellectual process, is one of the keys to effectively managing ethically complex situations.

Differentiation of self has nothing to do with changing other people. Rather, it has everything to do with improving one's own emotional functioning. Bowen says a more differentiated person can participate freely in the emotional sphere and also is free to shift to calm, logical reasoning for decisions that govern life" (as cited in Gilbert, 1992, p. 100). He says the critical stage in making such changes is passed "when the individual can begin to know the difference between emotional functioning and intellectual functioning, and when he has developed ways for using the knowledge for solving future problems in a lifelong effort of his own" (Bowen, 1988, as cited in Gilbert, 1992, p. 119).

Differentiation of self refers to a course in one's life, rather than a state of emotional detachment. As Friedman puts it, "It refers to the capacity to take a stand in an intense emotional environment. It means the capacity to say 'I' when others insist on 'we.' It refers to the capacity to avoid being polarized, to being a non-anxious presence in the presence of anxious others. It refers to being able to not automatically being one of the system's emotional dominoes, to being clear about your own values and goals, to taking maximum responsibility for your own emotional being and destiny rather than blaming others or the context" (1999, p. 236).

According to Nichols and Schwartz, "The differentiated person is capable of strong emotions and spontaneity, but also capable of the objectivity which comes with the ability to resist the pull of emotional responses" (1998, p. 140). Bowen's goal with his theory, and in his clinical practice, was to help people create a more differentiated self so they could become more responsible and higher-functioning individuals within the system or family. Kerr and Bowen (1988) state that a well-adjusted family unit allows each person his or her own feelings. In a well-adjusted social unit, maintaining a healthy social climate is more important than doing what others view as appropriate. Members of a well-adjusted social unit use each other as sources of learning, not as foils for comparative advantage, not as emotional crutches, and not as means toward others' ends.

SCHOOLS AS EMOTIONAL SYSTEMS

The first step in examining the upcoming case studies through the theoretical perspective of family systems theory is to recognize that the staff at a school, like a family, operates in an emotional system. This is easy to see in that schools share a number of features in common with the concept of family. As much as we might like to perceive ourselves as relatively autonomous people, we are linked physically, emotionally, and socially to others in our schools by many family-like features. Through some of the major components of our lives at school, such as having a principal whom we may like or dislike, dealing with decisions with which we agree or disagree, sharing duties and responsibilities, dealing with perceptions of favoritism, being involved with conflict with teachers down the hall, competing for resources and attention, enjoying positive staff morale or suffering negative school morale, engaging in constructive or destructive communication, dealing with trauma and crises, and not getting the class or schedule we wanted, schools and the people in them can be seen as operating as an emotional system.

There are also the students. Students, the major purpose and driver of our schools, connect us physically, emotionally, and socially. Our students are the reason we chose our careers. They are the people we work the hardest for. In effect, they are the people who are responsible for our jobs, our livelihoods.

Work is both noble and necessary for our well-being. Our work can create camaraderie and community. Our work provides income and the pleasures that it can buy. Lack of work, or even the threat of lack of work, can create insecurity. More often than the threat of the lack of work, organizational and interpersonal dynamics at work can create tension and anxiety.

We experience the constant tension between jobs and the security they provide, and the daily wear and tear they generate, such as commuting, managing new technology, maintaining our skills, trying to stay healthy, dealing with our students' academic and emotional issues, dealing with school and district bureaucracy, dealing with our students' parents, dealing with Child Protective Services, and, amid all that, trying to protect our personal time.

We experience the backbiting, the betrayal of confidences, and the unfairness in hiring. We experience the favoritism, the blind adherence to rules, or, perhaps, the selective interpretation of rules. We experience the bullying by colleagues, the unfair distribution of students, and the unfair distribution of scarce resources.

We all share in the more serious, anxiety-producing issues facing us, our families, and students, our whole world, in fact: the pervasive degradation of four things we all share and are dependent upon: our air, our soil, our water, and our global climate.

One of the tenets of family systems theory is that "when anxiety is high, people can become more reactive and less thoughtful; system functioning becomes prone to decline" (Bowen, 1978, p. 99). Typical school-based dynamics, and the resultant ethically complex situations, generally create a high degree of anxiety among teachers.

Family systems theory is based on eight interlocking concepts: the emotional system, levels of differentiation of self, mechanisms of reactivity in families, triangles, multigenerational transition processes, sibling position, anxiety, and emotional cut-off. We can see all of these dynamics playing out in our work in schools. In contrast to traditional theorists who placed individuals along a continuum from normal to dysfunctional, Bowen's family systems theory is based on the assumption that the interaction of these eight interlocking concepts will produce variation in human behavior within the family, and that the relationships between family members will have a significant impact on the total family unit.

This text joins others in applying family systems to schools. Friedman (1999) says the concept of emotional process can be applied to larger social systems, such as ethnic, national, and cultural groupings. Klicker says, "The way schools manage a crisis in the short term can negatively affect longer-term functioning" (2000, p. xx). In Cameron's application of Bowen's family systems model to the school setting, he explains that a school operates like a family system, with a series of subsystems that can influence the major system's functioning: "The term *system* refers to the relationship dynamics between school administration, staff, students, parents, and others within the formal organization" (2001, p. 1). A feature of all applications of family systems theory to schools is the attention paid to the emotional functioning of all the members in the system.

In ethically complex situations, as in most anxiety-producing situations, people's first reactions are often emotional. A primary physiological cause of such emotional reactions is the cortisol cascade of negative effects on human functioning.

THE CORTISOL CASCADE

When we are subject to threats, emotional danger, and times of high anxiety, our adrenal glands release a peptide called cortisol. Four of our body's immediate physical reactions to cortisol are the tensing of the large muscles in our body, an increase in our blood pressure, the shutting down of the higher levels of our cerebral functioning, and the depression of our immune system. These physical reactions lead to the reduction of our functioning to the well-known "fight or flight" response. More often, though, these physical reactions lead to the other and more common "f," *freeze*. More often than not, threats, physical or emotional danger, and times of high anxiety cause us to freeze, to not know what to do. Another common response to emotional threats and anxiety is resentment. We tend to resent those people and situations we encounter that create anxiety or emotional threat.

Threats and emotional danger activate our basic physiological defense mechanisms and behaviors that we know, through current research (Sapolsky, 2005), impede our higher functioning. The three major defense mechanisms and behaviors that are automatically activated by threats and emotional danger are fear, negative emotions, and emotional shut down. The negative emotions we experience tend to get remembered and associated with the person, the situation, or the event that causes the stress.

The stress associated with anxiety and emotional danger is a primary cause of poor functioning, emotional shut down, resentment, and depression. Some practical approaches for reducing stress associated with anxiety and emotional danger are to identify the causes, manage the conditions that can induce it, put names to the behaviors, and reduce these threats by establishing clear expectations about behaviors.

Research on behavior that leads to emotional danger indicates that the following *traditional* ways of dealing with it are *ineffective* and, in fact, contribute to the problem:

1. Telling people to ignore the situation or the person's behavior.
2. Saying that the event or the person's behavior is "just a phase."
3. Saying that the person's behavior is just "that person's way of communicating."
4. Telling people to not be so sensitive to such events or behavior.
5. Tolerating such events or people's behavior and hoping things will get better.

Research on, and long-standing clinical understanding of, behavior that leads to emotional danger indicates that the following ways of dealing with it are *highly effective*:

1. Confronting the behavior.
2. Putting a name to the behavior.
3. Informing people that they do not have to put up with it.
4. Saying, "I do not like what you are doing."
5. Identifying the requested change in behavior.

EMOTIONS

Why pay attention to emotions, especially during tense and ethically complex situations? Because emotions drive our attention: they create meaning for us; they create their own memory pathways and reinforce what we think about people, places, and events. Emotions are universal: they are biologically generated and result in pleasure, fear, surprise, disgust, anger, and sadness. Another reason we should pay attention to our emotions, especially during stressful and ethically complex situations, is because emotions are a significant element of our personalities.

We can increase our ability to navigate through tense and ethically complex situations in a number of ways. We can focus our awareness on the present. We can create ways to establish calm before responding in difficult or anxious situations. We can be more aware of the types of choices we tend to make. We can be more conscious of the array of responses available to us, and by deliberately blending our thinking and our feeling in order to generate better decisions.

As Goleman (1995) and Mayer and Salovey (1997) point out, being aware of and responsive to one's emotions does not mean merely "being nice." It means consciously and carefully processing and using one's emotional information and emotional energy.

As the learning activities ask, as the case studies demonstrate, and as the reflection and discussion questions point out, we can accomplish emotional awareness by identifying our emotional status. We can ask ourselves: "What do I feel about this? What might the other person feel?" We can use our emotions to help our thinking. We can ask ourselves: "Is this mood helpful? Does it help me focus my attention on a resolution of the situation, or does it create a bigger problem?" We can understand the source and history of our emotions by asking ourselves, "Why am I feeling this way?" "Have I felt this way before?" "How will I feel if I continue in this direction?" Engaging in these kinds of self-awareness questions can help us do a more effective job of managing our emotions and balancing them with how our intellect informs us.

Some of the positive outcomes of such emotional awareness questions include a deeper awareness of more effective decision making due to realizing what is behind our decisions. Another positive outcome is that such self-questioning can lead to looking at actions with their consequences in mind. And, finally, such emotional awareness typically results in more effective management of our feelings—by realizing what lies behind our feelings, we can reduce our negative self-talk and better understand how to handle our fears and anxieties.

What makes people operate the way they do? What happens when people face difficult options? As stated in the introduction, examining ourselves—why we do what we do—is the very essence of human psychology . . . and of ethics.

REFLECTION AND DISCUSSION QUESTIONS

1. What kinds of emotions were most present in the household you grew up in?
2. How did your parents deal with anxiety and stressful situations?
3. How do you tend to deal with anxiety and stressful situations?
4. Do you find that you deal with anxiety and stressful situations the same, or differently, in a variety of settings, such as at home, at work, in other groups?

5. To the degree that you have experienced backbiting, betrayal of confidences, unfairness in hiring, favoritism, selective interpretation of rules, or bullying by colleagues, how have you handled them?

6. Describe a situation in which you have experienced the *freeze* effect, the not knowing what to do, of the cortisol cascade.

7. Can you identify any experiences of poor functioning, emotional shut down, resentment, and/or depression associated with anxiety or stressful events and the cortisol cascade?

8. Describe your internal responses to being told "ignore the situation," "ignore the person's behavior," "it's just a phase," "it's just that person's way of communicating," "don't be so sensitive," or "it's okay, things will get better."

9. Knowing that one of our goals is to be more conscious of the array of responses available to us and to deliberately blend our thinking and our feeling in order to generate better decisions, describe an event in the past that you would now handle differently.

10

A Story about Confidentiality

My naïveté caused me to bring this upon myself. I'm a pretty cheerful, talkative guy, and I was duped by an innocent comment. I'm now more guarded about what I say and to whom, and I never discuss students in public places. This situation has humbled me and made me a more reflective and thoughtful teacher.

William

William was recently hired to teach fourth grade at Saint Katherine School in the community of Mendoza Springs. As a new teacher in an unfamiliar community, it took some time for William to gain an understanding of the students and parents that he and his colleagues were serving.

William had a student, Melinda, in his fourth grade class. Melinda had just recently moved to the community, so she did not have any previously established friends in the class. Melinda was a quiet, shy girl who was eager to please. She had a younger brother in first grade, and through the month's early religion classes, based on the topic "My Family," William learned that Melinda's mom and dad were divorced. When William first met Melinda's mother at the oral interviews in October, her air of self-confidence struck him. She drove a big, new, apparently expensive SUV. She dressed in designer clothes, which is not typical in Mendoza Springs. She seemed quite intimidating, and William had a difficult time establishing a rapport with her.

THE SITUATION

As part of the fourth-grade curricula for physical education and health, the students are required to take swimming lessons. Melinda's mother wrote a lengthy letter to William to explain Melinda's skin condition and Melinda's embarrassment when wearing a bathing suit. Even so, William spoke to Melinda and encouraged her to participate, which she did quite readily. The swimming classes proceeded and there were no further discussions of Melinda's skin condition.

In November, William went to a regularly scheduled dental appointment. As he paid his bill, the receptionist commented casually that she knew a student in William's room and that she was a friend of the student's father. That student was Melinda. William had not met Melinda's father. In a brief, casual response to her comment about knowing Melinda's father, William stated how he had seen great progress with Melinda's confidence and in her ability to make friends, and that he was very proud of her for swimming, when he knew she was feeling somewhat shy about it due to her skin condition. At the time, there was no one else present in the reception area.

Within days, it became clear that the receptionist was more than a friend of Melinda's father. She was his girlfriend, and William's innocent comments would be taken out of context and used against him.

A few days later, William received a terse note from Melinda's mother informing him of his breach of confidentiality. She stated that if William had any information regarding her daughter, he was to share it with her and not to discuss it with her ex-husband's current girlfriend. William was stunned. He planned to tell his principal of his dilemma at recess or lunchtime. However, when he saw Melinda's mother arrive at school at 9:30 AM, he knew he was going to be the *second* person to tell the principal the story.

William was summoned to see the principal at the 10:00 morning recess. William apologized to the principal for not telling her of the note as soon as he had received it so she could have been prepared for Melinda's mother, who was extremely irate about her daughter's personal issues being discussed in a public place. The principal supported William without having heard his side of the story. She assured Melinda's mother that it was not like William to discuss personal information about students, and she vouched for his high moral standard. Melinda's mother was adamant that William be reprimanded and punished for discussing her daughter's personal information with anyone besides her. The principal told her she would speak with William, but that discipline measures would be unlikely.

WILLIAM'S EMOTIONAL RESPONSE

William felt sick inside because he knew he might have said too much to a non-parent about a student in his room. He was only in his third year of teaching, but he knew he should not be sharing information about students entrusted to his care, to an unknown person, especially in a public place.

He was also very angry. He felt tricked by the receptionist and her use of the information he had casually mentioned to her. Even though he had erred, he felt deceived.

He was embarrassed when Melinda's mother confronted him with the information he had said to the receptionist. She quoted him almost word for word of what he had said at the dentist's office. He was also feeling defensive about his role in the situation.

He was pleased by his principal's support. He felt lucky he had worked with her enough for her to attest to his level of integrity and know his outgoing nature, as well as to know he was a professional with regard to confidential student information.

WILLIAM'S INTELLECTUAL RESPONSE

William knows he was wrong to have divulged personal information about a student to a non-parent. He was relieved when the principal exonerated him with nothing more than a gentle reminder about proper professional protocol. He knew that according to his professional code of conduct, he could have been in trouble if the principal or the mother felt the matter should be taken to the next disciplinary level.

William knows the receptionist took the information gained from him, shared it with her boyfriend, perhaps to gain favor with him, and then passed it on to the mother, perhaps with the intention of trying to discredit her in some way. The mother reacted emotionally because she was protective of her child, and she felt William should have shared the information with her rather than create a situation in which she heard about it secondhand. Intellectually, William knew he might have reacted similarly had Melinda been his child.

William knows that in order for the principal to be effective in her position, she needs open and honest communication with her teachers to properly support them. William acknowledges that he put the principal in a difficult position. He should have forewarned her about what had happened, so she could have better prepared herself for the meeting with Melinda's mother.

WILLIAM'S ACTIONS

William called Melinda's mother and spoke to her directly about the situation. He apologized for not having shared the information with her first, although nothing that he had said to the receptionist had been any different from what he had discussed with the mother at the oral interview in October, except for the situation surrounding Melinda's sensitivity about her skin condition. He told her that his casual comments had been used against him for her own personal gain or to cause a fight.

William also called the receptionist and told her of the great difficulties she had brought upon him. She was apologetic for her actions and did not have any justification for what she had done. She knew what he had said had been under the assumption that it was not going any further than an empty dentist's office.

FORCES AFFECTING THE SITUATION

William says there was a strong force of parental protection acting in this situation. A confident woman, feeling undermined by her husband's girlfriend with regard to issues surrounding her child, is a significant force. There were also the forces of a difficult divorce whose repercussions were felt in his classroom. Had the same comment been made in a situation where the mother and girlfriend were on good terms, William does not see that he would have faced this problem. There was tension, and he found himself caught in the middle of it.

His exuberant naiveté caused him to bring this upon himself because he did not understand the relationship between Melinda's father and the receptionist. William says he is a cheerful, talkative person who feels that he was duped, by an innocent comment, into having to make a visit to the principal's office. He feels that his general level of trust has been shaken after this incident.

Finally, the principal who negotiated the situation was a guiding force. She defended William, counseled him, disciplined him, and believed in him when he needed her. This memory of her full support remains as a constant reminder of her ability to advocate for her teachers.

CONCLUSION

Since that time, William has been guarded about what he says and to whom. He never discusses students in public places, and if he ever tells a story about a student, he does not use the real name. William says this situation has humbled him and made him a more reflective and thoughtful teacher.

REFLECTION AND DISCUSSION QUESTIONS: PRACTICAL AND PROFESSIONAL ETHICS

1. Has William violated his student's confidentiality?
2. Do teachers have ethical responsibilities for confidentiality about their students?
3. How might Hume's response to the first question be different from Downie and Telfer's?
4. What are your thoughts about the manner in which the mother handled the situation?
5. Do teachers have ethical responsibilities regarding parents' concerns for their children?
6. What do you think about the way in which the principal handled the situation?

REFLECTION AND DISCUSSION QUESTIONS: DIFFERENTIATION OF SELF

1. William describes himself as a cheerful, talkative guy. Does this type of personality present any special challenges in managing one's self in complex situations?
2. William said he felt sick inside, tricked, and embarrassed. To the degree you have ever felt these emotions in a complex situation, how have they affected your ability to handle the situation?
3. William also says that since the situation, he has been guarded about what he says and to whom. How would you explain this response with what you know about the cortisol cascade?
4. If you were in this or a similar situation, instead of going from cheerful and talkative to embarrassed and guarded, how might you work toward the objectivity needed to resist the pull of these emotional responses?
5. How might you adjust to being a new teacher looking to build relationships in a new community?

11

Professional Ethics, Moral Values, and Confidentiality

It is my professional responsibility to uphold the confidentiality between teachers, parents, and students. I also have a moral responsibility to advocate for the welfare of a child. My moral responsibility outweighed my professional responsibility.

Mr. Brian

Everyone has a set of values that they hold to be true. These are the principles by which we set the standards for our behavior. Sometimes circumstances occur that create a conflict of our values and principles, placing us in a situation of ethical compromise. This is the situation in Mr. Brian's dilemma.

THE SITUATION

Aaron was a student in Mr. Brian's fifth-grade class. Aaron and his younger sister, Lauren, who was in second grade, were new to the school. Aaron was polite and cooperative in the classroom. He made friends easily. However, on the playground, Aaron was quick to anger and was involved in numerous physical conflicts with other students. Aaron tended to bully younger children. His file indicated that these behaviors had been a pattern in the past couple of years.

Aaron's father, Phil, requested an interview with Mr. Brian early in the school year. In the interview, Phil outlined the family background. There was a history of alcohol abuse, drug abuse, and domestic violence. Aaron had witnessed physical and verbal fights between his parents. Aaron's mother had been physically abusive to him. The mother left the family about two years ago and was believed to be living on the streets in a larger city nearby. Phil admitted to Mr. Brian that he was having difficulty coping as a single parent. Various social service agencies were involved with the family, but Phil's main support had come from his parents. Several times in the past, Phil's parents had been given custody of Aaron and Lauren. In the desire to give everyone a fresh start, Phil's parents had recently set Phil up in an apartment near the school. Phil had been through an alcohol treatment program. He was also taking courses at the local community college.

Over the next few months, Phil frequently came to the school to discuss Aaron's progress with Mr. Brian. During some of these visits, Phil expressed concern about Aaron's behavior at home. Phil told Mr. Brian that Aaron had frequent outbursts of anger and that he would react violently to a variety of things by hitting, screaming, and kicking. Phil said that most often, Aaron directed his violence toward his younger sister, Lauren. Phil said that Aaron was becoming more difficult for him to control. As a result, Phil's parents began having either Aaron or Lauren stay with them on weekends in order to separate them. Phil told Mr. Brian that he would like some help in arranging counseling for Aaron.

Mr. Brian had a friend, Janet. Janet was a single parent. One day after Christmas break, Mr. Brian saw Janet in the office at school. Janet was registering her daughter for Kindergarten. Mr. Brian and Janet began chatting, and Janet told Mr. Brian that she had moved into the apartment complex near the school. Janet was starting a new job that would involve shift work with some evenings and nights. Janet told Mr. Brian that she had met a man in her apartment complex, a single parent whose two kids attended this school. They had become friends, and this other single parent had offered to look after Janet's daughter while she worked. The other single parent would even let Janet's daughter stay overnight when Janet worked night shift, and he would take her to school with his own two children on those mornings. The other single parent Janet was talking about was Phil.

Mr. Brian says this turn of events created a dilemma for him. Mr. Brian did not believe that Phil could safely provide care for Janet's daughter. However, his opinion was based on knowledge he had gained as a result of his professional relationship with Phil and Aaron, and this teacher/student/parent relationship carried with it an expectation of professional confidentiality. For Mr. Brian to explain to Janet his concerns about Phil's suitability to take care of Janet's daughter would be a breach of confidentiality, which, according to his professional ethics, would be wrong. Yet, not telling Janet would be morally wrong because Mr. Brian believed that the welfare of Janet's daughter could be jeopardized if Phil were to become her babysitter. Mr. Brian believed that he was in a situation where he had to choose between his professional ethics and his moral values.

MR. BRIAN'S EMOTIONAL RESPONSE

Mr. Brian reports that his first emotional response to this situation was extreme discomfort. He had a difficult decision to make. He respected the need for confidentiality between teachers and their students and parents, and he also believed in Phil's right to privacy. However, he also believed that Janet had a right to fully understand the situation in which she was placing her daughter. Mr. Brian was terribly uncomfortable in having to choose one of these beliefs over the other.

Mr. Brian was also uncomfortable with how the choice he would make would reflect on him personally and professionally. If he chose to keep the information confidential, Janet could well discover that Mr. Brian had not advised her of the potential harm to her daughter. If Mr. Brian chose to inform Janet, Phil and other parents, could find out that he had shared confidential information. In either case, Mr. Brian felt that someone would lose trust and confidence in him.

Mr. Brian says that as he thought more about the situation, he became angry with Phil for offering to take care of another person's child when he had difficulty taking care of his own children. Phil had told Mr. Brian that he had felt the need to have his own children separated for the safety of his daughter, yet here he was, willing to have another person's child brought into his home.

MR. BRIAN'S INTELLECTUAL RESPONSE

Mr. Brian struggled with a variety of issues and points of view. The first one was that this situation was none of his business. But Mr. Brian also believed that the welfare of children is everyone's business. On the other hand, Janet had not asked for Mr. Brian's opinion. Janet had expressed no concern about Phil or Aaron. Mr. Brian also suspected that if he had not known Phil's family history, he might not have entertained any thought of questioning Janet's choice. If that were the case, Mr. Brian would not have given their conversation a second thought.

The reality was that Mr. Brian did have knowledge of Phil's difficult family history and present situation. If Janet did not have this knowledge, Mr. Brian felt that he had a moral responsibility to share it with her because it was relevant to her daughter's welfare.

MR. BRIAN'S ACTIONS

Mr. Brian decided that he would first determine if Janet had any knowledge of Phil's home situation. If she did, Mr. Brian would make no comment nor would he offer an opinion. He would not need to go against his professional ethics. If Janet did not have this knowledge, then Mr. Brian thought he should share the information he had, but only to the extent that was needed for Janet to make an informed decision for the care and safety of her child.

Mr. Brian contacted Janet. During the course of their conversation, it was apparent that Janet had no knowledge of Phil's family background or of Aaron's behavioral problems. Mr. Brian first explained that he was passing on some confidential information out of concern for Janet's daughter, and that he felt very uncomfortable about discussing it. Mr. Brian disclosed only the parts of the information that he thought pertained directly to the safety and welfare of Janet's child: Aaron's behavioral problems with other children at school and the concerns Phil had about Aaron's violent outbursts at home. Mr. Brian also told Janet that Phil was seeking professional help for Aaron. Mr. Brian did not discuss the events that had occurred in Phil's past. Mr. Brian made no suggestion or recommendation about a course of action that Janet should take. Mr. Brian says that Janet thanked him for the information, and that they did not discuss Phil or Aaron again.

The next time he saw Phil, Mr. Brian was very uncomfortable. However, Phil showed no indication that he knew of Mr. Brian's conversation with Janet. Mr. Brian did learn that Janet had arranged to have another sitter come into her home while she worked night shift. After spring break, Aaron and Lauren transferred to another school.

FORCES AFFECTING THE SITUATION

Mr. Brian can identify three forces that were acting on this situation. The first force was that Mr. Brian had known Janet personally. Mr. Brian says that if he had not known her, he would not have learned that Phil was considering babysitting another child. Therefore, he would not have been in this situation of ethical compromise.

The other two forces were internal forces. The first was the expectation Mr. Brian had of himself as a professional. Mr. Brian says he felt that it was his responsibility to uphold the confidentiality between teachers, parents, and students. The relationship a teacher has with students and parents should be based on trust. If Mr. Brian violated that trust, he knew he would lose credibility as a teacher, not only with the students and parents, but also with himself. The second force was the expectation he had of himself as a member of society. Mr. Brian believes that he has a moral responsibility to advocate for the welfare of any child.

This situation created a conflict of two values and caused an ethical compromise for Mr. Brian. In making his decision, he felt that his moral responsibility outweighed his professional responsibility. By disclosing the confidential information he had about Phil and Aaron, he believes that he would possibly be preventing the risk of harm to Janet's daughter. It was a difficult choice for him to make, but in the end, given the circumstances, he believes that he made the right decision.

REFLECTION AND DISCUSSION QUESTIONS: PRACTICAL AND PROFESSIONAL ETHICS

1. How might Kant and Mill respond to this situation?
2. Put yourself in Janet's position. Do you think Mr. Brian did the right thing?
3. Put yourself in Phil's position. Do you think Mr. Brian did the right thing?
4. Would it make a difference in this case if Janet's child were a boy in fifth grade rather than a girl in second grade?
5. Was anyone hurt by the way Mr. Brian handled this situation?
6. Can you think of any point is this case at which Mr. Brian might have rightfully been expected to seek advice from someone else at school? If so, who?
7. Could talking about such a situation with a colleague be seen as a breach of confidentiality?
8. If you were the school principal, and Mr. Brian came to you for advice about this situation, how would you have advised Mr. Brian?
9. What do you think about Mr. Brian's idea that one's moral responsibility toward protecting children outweighs one's professional responsibility of confidentiality toward students and parents?

REFLECTION AND DISCUSSION QUESTIONS: DIFFERENTIATION OF SELF

1. Mr. Brian said he was uncomfortable with how his choice would reflect on him personally and professionally. Explain why you think teachers should or should not be concerned about how others view them.
2. Can teachers, or anyone else, control how others view them?
3. Is it possible for teachers to act in such a way that nobody would lose trust and confidence in them?

4. Mr. Brian says he became angry with Phil for offering to take care of another person's child when he had difficulty taking care of his own children. Knowing that a teacher's professional practice is filled with people who do things that we do not agree with, how might you protect yourself from becoming perpetually angry or, even worse, burned out, without becoming uncaring or unconcerned?

12

Confidences Betrayed: The Pain Flows In and Out in Waves

I didn't want to be part of the problem. I made a mistake in sharing my concerns in the first place. I compromised my own code of ethics by doing so. I had not been this aware of the ramifications of the ethics of my profession for a long time.

Janelle

Janelle began talking about her situation by saying, "We are all responsible for our choices, and we have a duty to make choices in a morally responsible way. This is especially important when we have power and influence over the lives of others, as is the case with school administrators and the teachers they lead."

THE SITUATION

It was Friday afternoon and Janelle had been thinking back over the past few weeks about the unanticipated complexities of her job, when Theresa, her principal, came over to her and greeted her as she was doing some photocopying. The two of them exchanged pleasantries, and Janelle noticed that Theresa seemed nervous. Theresa's eyes scanned the hallway and returned to Janelle. What Theresa then said surprised and worried Janelle, and Janelle realized why Theresa appeared to be so edgy. Theresa alluded to Janelle's earlier, private conversation with her about Janelle's experience of an ethical dilemma involving a colleague who was still teaching at that school. Janelle had discretely asked Theresa about the situation. Although

Janelle had used pseudonyms throughout the discussion, Theresa knew of whom Janelle was speaking: Monique, a fourth-grade teacher.

Now, Theresa, the principal, said that there were two fourth-grade teachers in the school who were struggling to make a difficult decision. They had to decide whether they would file a formal complaint against a teacher. This teacher, Monique, was harassing them and accusing them of picking on her. Theresa suggested, in a hushed tone, that if Janelle spoke to them about her own experiences with this teacher, it might help them make the difficult decision to go ahead and file a formal complaint against Monique. Apparently, the other two teachers had followed the union protocols up to this point, and now the administration and the teachers association were involved. The way Theresa presented the suggestion reminded Janelle of secretive meetings in smoky back rooms, where names are not mentioned, but everyone is aware of the person who is going to be snuffed out. It seemed to Janelle that Theresa and the other two teachers were hoping that she, Janelle, would be their hit man.

Administrators sometimes find themselves in the role of the bad guy. They are decision makers, leaders, organizers, and facilitators for teachers, parents, and students. Many of these administrative responsibilities have an ethical component to them, and when administrators make decisions they must do so fairly and justly. When administrators evaluate teachers, they must be fair and compassionate. Administrators face difficult choices when they find themselves in a situation where a teacher has been behaving unethically or is seen to be incompetent in some way. They must find a way to help and support the teacher or minimize the potential harm to the students by finding a way to get the teacher out of the classroom. At least this is what Janelle believed.

Janelle knew that Monique had, for over a decade, received mixed ratings by the administration. Her file contained several letters from distressed and unhappy parents whose children had been in her class and had experienced her unstable personality. Over the years, Monique struggled with many demons and faced many challenges of life including divorce, financial difficulties, and serious legal, drug-related problems with her son. Monique loved teaching and she considered herself to be a person of integrity, but she was frustrated by her constant array of problems and her apparent inability to fit in with others at this school.

Theresa is a highly organized and purposeful woman. She worked hard to make the school a quality school in every way. Faced with the ongoing frustration of having to deal with Monique, irate parents, annoyed teachers, and uncertain students, Theresa was at the stage of pulling out her hair and wanting the problem to go away. Janelle believes that Theresa's frustration with the apparent insolvability of the "Monique problem," coupled with Theresa's goal of running a top-notch school, became the precursors for this ethical dilemma.

The problem would certainly be solved if enough evidence could be gathered to show that Monique should not be teaching. Janelle believes that Theresa was at a point with this issue where she saw this latest incident with the other fourth-grade teachers as a way to put the final nail in Monique's coffin, and she wanted to have as much support as possible. What Theresa now remembered were the experiences that Janelle had had teaching with Monique. Janelle further believes that Theresa saw Janelle as a person who might support her and the other two teachers in their quest to get Monique out of teaching, and out of their school, once and for all. Desperate times, it seemed, called for desperate measures.

JANELLE'S EMOTIONAL RESPONSES

Janelle felt a bit desperate herself and strong feelings flooded her when she first heard what Theresa was suggesting. Janelle was initially confused, but when it became clear to her what Theresa wanted, Janelle was offended and upset that Theresa thought Janelle would do something like that. Janelle felt betrayed because she had shared her earlier thoughts and concerns with Theresa, believing they would be confidential and that Theresa would respect the fact that the purpose of her shared comments was to look for potential solutions, especially given that Janelle had talked about how she had tried to help Monique overcome some of her problems. In fact, just sharing these thoughts now makes Janelle angry. At the time of the conversation with Theresa, however, Janelle was able to hold her emotions in check because she sensed that both she and Theresa knew they were skirting the edge of ethical quicksand simply by talking about a colleague's professional practice. But now, Janelle just stood there and hoped she would be able to find the right thing to say.

JANELLE'S INTELLECTUAL RESPONSES

Janelle's thoughts ran in many directions. On the one hand, she had an appreciation for the difficult nature of the situation. Holding a person's future in your hands is a huge responsibility, and it requires delicate handling. Theresa's concern for the students and families, as well as for Monique, was evident in her efforts to find a solution that would result in a win-win situation for all those involved. On the other hand, Janelle knew that Theresa had compromised her code of ethics in several ways. She had revealed confidential information about Janelle's colleagues and, as such, was not respecting the rights of all individuals, Janelle included. Theresa was also entrusted to promote quality leadership in education and meet her professional responsibilities with honesty and integrity. She was not being a positive role model or a good leader in these circumstances. Theresa is a proactive person and she would want to deal with the issue and get on to helping create a positive school environment. As such, Janelle could see how Theresa would feel somewhat thwarted by the problems she was having with Monique.

JANELLE'S ACTIONS

Janelle did not want to become part of the problem. Janelle asked Theresa if the two of them could speak privately in her office. Safely behind closed doors, Janelle acknowledged the frustrations that Theresa must be experiencing, and she commented on the fact that she knew Theresa had the best interests of the students and Monique at heart. Janelle said that she felt she had made a mistake in sharing her earlier concerns in the first place, and that she had possibly compromised her own code of ethics by doing so. It would be unethical, she told Theresa, to pass on confidential information about her colleague. Janelle told Theresa that she could not do what Theresa wanted and that she hoped Theresa would be able to find another way to solve the problems she was facing with Monique. Janelle left the conversation thinking that she had not been this aware of the ramifications of the ethics of her profession for a long time.

Looking back on this experience, Janelle says she recognizes that Theresa must attend to what is the greatest good for the greatest number, and, at the same time, she must show respect to all persons involved. Now, as Janelle goes about her daily duties as a teacher, she says that her awareness of the many ethical situations she encounters every day is heightened as a result of reflecting on this incident.

Janelle says she feels that in some ways she understands the situation and the people involved more fully now. Monique, Theresa, and Janelle, she can see now, are struggling: Monique to maintain her dignity and her integrity, Theresa to fulfill the responsibilities of her job, and Janelle to keep her promises of confidentiality. In many ways, they are using the only skills they have. Janelle is empathetic because even if the situation is handled properly, it will exact a considerable emotional toll on both of them.

REFLECTION AND DISCUSSION QUESTIONS: PRACTICAL AND PROFESSIONAL ETHICS

1. Describe how various theorists might respond to talking about colleagues in the way described here.

2. Janelle says Theresa revealed confidential information about Janelle's colleagues and, as such, was not respecting the rights of all individuals. Do administrators have the right to confide in colleagues?
3. Explain why you do or do not think this is a good example of attending to the greatest good for the greatest number.
4. If you were Monique, how would you want this situation to be dealt with?

REFLECTION AND DISCUSSION QUESTIONS: DIFFERENTIATION OF SELF

1. Janelle noticed that Theresa seemed nervous. What Theresa said surprised and worried Janelle, and Janelle realized why Theresa appeared to be so edgy. What kinds of clues are present in this situation that might give notice that someone is trying to pull another person into an emotional entanglement or, as family systems theory would say, *triangulation*?
2. What do you think of Janelle's telling Theresa that she felt she had made a mistake in sharing her earlier concerns in the first place, that she had possibly compromised her own code of ethics by doing so, and that it would be unethical to pass on confidential information about her colleague?
3. Describe a situation in which you either admitted a mistake, or wish you had, in talking about other people. What kinds of emotions were, or would be, involved?

13

Inappropriate Relationships

I've never been content with my reaction to this moral dilemma. I witnessed inappropriate behavior, but who was I, a first-year teacher, to question a colleague's behavior? This incident forced me to re-evaluate my own values and ethics. I feel certain that if I faced a similar situation, I would not be so cautious in making those tough decisions.

Barbara

Every day, teachers are faced with the overwhelming task of making difficult decisions. Inevitably, one's own personal values and beliefs play an integral role in this decision-making process. Doing the right thing appears to be easy, but with many ethical dilemmas, overcoming the barrier that separates belief from action involves confrontation and controversy—thus making indecision the more common course of action.

THE SITUATION

Barbara was a first-year teacher. She taught in a small, rural high school in a community that was proud of its students' academic and athletic success. Barbara was eager to become involved in the extra-curricular aspects of school life, so she immediately accepted the position of head coach for the junior girls' basketball team. A fellow colleague, Larry, coached the senior girls' team. Larry was a 24-year-old male who loved the game. He played basketball in high school and college. Now, as a third-year teacher and coach, he devoted countless hours to preparing his team for the State Championship games.

Lisa was one of the exceptional players on the senior girls' team. She was also a source of pride in the community due to her story of adversity, effort, and personal accomplishment. When she was 12 years old, a drunk driver plowed into her while she was walking home from school. Her legs, hip, and spine were severely damaged. She missed a year of school due to her injuries and surgeries. She and her family were told by doctors that she would probably never walk again. Yet, here she was—not only was she walking, she was playing high school basketball at a highly competitive level. She was also likely to get a scholarship at a nearby university with an outstanding women's team.

Early in the season, a rumor surfaced within the school and the community that Larry was having a sexual relationship with one of his players. The school staff was aware that Larry spent a lot of time with Lisa, but the idea that he would take advantage of his position of trust and power seemed absurd to everyone. Barbara felt certain that the extra time Larry spent with Lisa was innocent and that his motives were genuine, as he mentored her toward her goal of playing basketball at the college level.

That season, the basketball coaching staff traveled to a weekend coaching clinic at a university in a nearby city. Lisa had been in telephone contact with the head coach of that university because she was working toward a scholarship there. So, it made sense that Lisa would travel with Larry and the rest of the coaching staff to meet face-to-face with the person who would likely be her future coach.

Up to this time, Barbara had never witnessed any type of behavior between Larry and Lisa that she would have regarded as inappropriate. She sided with many of her colleagues who felt that Larry was the target of rumors because he was a young, single teacher who coached a female sports team, and that small-town mentality was probably the source of most of the stories.

However, throughout the course of the weekend-coaching clinic, Barbara observed that the level of affection Larry displayed toward Lisa was close to, if not over, the line of appropriateness for a teacher. Barbara cared a great deal for all of her players and most of her students, but she could not fathom holding hands or snuggling with any of them. She felt very awkward, uncomfortable, and totally unsure about how to handle the types of affectionate behavior she saw between Larry and Lisa. Barbara was also angry with Larry; when community members asked about his relationship with Lisa, Barbara had always been quick to defend his actions as being genuine, caring, and professional. Now, she was forced to wonder if she had been wrong in protecting him against the rumors.

Upon returning to school, some of the people who had traveled to the coaching clinic met to discuss the weekend. The conversation and opinions about Larry's behavior wavered back and forth, and the only decision people could agree upon was to make the principal aware of what they had observed, hoping that the principal could help guide them through this unfamiliar and uncomfortable territory. Barbara felt comfortable with their decision; surely, the school principal would advise them as to whether Larry's actions were inappropriate. Barbara felt a sense of relief that the problem was now in the hands of her superior, because he would thoroughly investigate the matter and take whatever steps were necessary to remedy the situation.

Eventually, meetings with Larry were held at the school level and the school-board level, with and without union representation. Through it all, Larry denied any type of inappropriate actions on his part. The school board gave Larry strict orders to avoid any and all contact with Lisa. As the month of June drew to a close, people could cut the tension in the school with a knife. Two camps emerged: students, parents, community members, and staff who questioned why nothing was being done to or about Larry; and a second camp of similar make-up that supported Larry. The end of the year came with Larry announcing that he was going to seek employment in another part of the state. Larry never returned to Barbara's community, but the issue over his relationship with a student opened a wound on her school's staff that has not healed.

BARBARA'S RESPONSE

They say hindsight is 20–20. In this case, Barbara can attest that it certainly is true. She has never been content with her reaction to this moral dilemma. She knows that, as a teacher, she carries a lot of power and influence with her students, and even more so with her athletes. Barbara realizes that she witnessed inappropriate behavior, but she took the easy route out, choosing to leave the principal and the school board to deal with a very sensitive situation. But who was she, a first-year teacher in the school, to openly question another colleague's behavior? Barbara feels that as a school district, including the principal, the superintendent, and the coaching staff, they let the system and their students down. She says they were happy to have Larry out of the district, sweeping the whole messy situation under the carpet, because that was much easier than the publicity and controversy that would certainly have followed if they had pushed for further investigation.

These few years later, Barbara says she recognizes that she had no control over how the school administration or school board dealt with this issue, but she did have control over her actions. Given the time back, she says she would have taken her concerns directly to the superintendent of public instruction. The incident forced her to re-evaluate her own values and ethics, and, as a result, she feels certain that if she faced a similar situation, she would not be so cautious in making those tough decisions. Barbara says she owes it to her students and to the members of her staff to always take the higher moral road, leading by example every step of the way. As an endnote, Larry and Lisa married each other this past summer. Both of them are certified teachers and work in a larger town nearby.

REFLECTION AND DISCUSSION QUESTIONS: PRACTICAL AND PROFESSIONAL ETHICS

1. Nearly all standards of teachers' professional ethics stipulate that the power differential between teacher and student is so great, any fraternization not only is suspect, it is wrong. Nearly all states have laws that prohibit sexual contact between teacher and student. Yet, incidents like this are reported with increasing regularity. Why do you think that is? What is your recommendation to the profession to help keep this type of situation from occurring?
2. Given that you care a great deal for your students, would you hold hands with any of them?
3. Barbara says Larry and Lisa married each other and that both of them are certified teachers and work in a larger town nearby. How might Hume respond to this situation?
4. Regardless of how the situation turned out, how might Rand, Kant, and Plato respond to this situation?

REFLECTION AND DISCUSSION QUESTIONS: DIFFERENTIATION OF SELF

1. What is your emotional reaction to this situation?
2. What is your intellectual reaction to this situation?
3. When tensions run high about an issue, people in the school community usually do get involved and express their opinions, often in camps, as this situation shows. They often try and pull people to their point of view, or criticize and, perhaps, ostracize people for not sharing the same point of view as their camp. Describe a situation in which you have been a part of such a camp or have been criticized or ostracized for not being part of such a camp.
4. What did you learn about yourself from that situation?

14

Blind Adherence to School Policies and Child Protective Services?

The solution is rarely black and white.

Randy

In his first year of teaching, Randy met a boy named Jake. Jake was a seventh-grader in another class, but Randy taught Jake physical education, and he supervised Jake on the middle school's sports teams, as well as on the school grounds before and after the school day began. Jake presented an array of behavior issues. He didn't show severe behavioral problems, but he was frequently caught being off school grounds during the day, engaging in rough play, teasing other students, and, on occasion, being disrespectful of noon-hour supervisors and teachers.

THE SITUATION

One day, Jake came to school clearly in a bad mood. Right away, he broke three of the school's rules, and he was not responding well to the consequence Randy gave him. In cases such as this, the next step would be to contact a parent to take the student home for the day. Unfortunately, calling Jake's father could create other problems. Although Randy was aware of the school and district policies dealing with students who present behavioral problems, he wondered if these policies addressed the emotional needs of this particular student.

RANDY'S EMOTIONAL RESPONSE

Though Jake was sometimes a problem at the school, Randy had a bit of a soft spot for him. Randy knew that Jake's behavior was, to some extent, a plea for attention because of a less than ideal home life. Jake's parents were divorced, and he was living with his biological father who was known by the school's teachers and administrators to be extremely strict. Complicating the matter further was the fact that Jake's father overreacted when the school contacted him recently about his son's behavior. Jake's father would often come to the school and yell at Jake, and there were some hints of emotional and physical abuse. There was no outward evidence of physical abuse, but Jake's body language when around his father indicated genuine fear.

Therefore, the dilemma was how to handle this new situation with Jake. Randy was afraid that there was an element of risk for Jake if he contacted Jake's dad. However, if Randy contacted Child Protective Services (CPS), and it turned out his suspicions of physical abuse were false, then the family could be unnecessarily embarrassed, and Randy and the school could lose whatever remained of their support and trust with Jake and his dad. Whatever decision Randy made, he had to consider all the factors involved and not disregard school and district policy and procedure for dealing with Jake's problematic behavior.

RANDY'S INTELLECTUAL RESPONSE

All emotions aside, the logical solution was to follow through with due process consistent with any other student. If Randy showed leniency for Jake, then the other students would notice the inconsistencies, which would generate another set of problems. Also, the law clearly states that teachers must report any suspicions of child abuse or neglect to either the police or to CPS. Teachers are not supposed to investigate the matter, but instead turn it over completely to the police or to CPS. In order to make the best possible decision in this situation, Randy felt he had to follow district policy and procedure, but also consider the reality of Jake's emotional well-being.

RANDY'S ACTIONS

After careful consideration of all the factors, Randy finally decided to talk to Jake to learn more about what had caused his misbehavior that morning, and to try to gain a better understanding of his relationship with his father. Randy knew that he might not have been following proper protocol, but he felt he owed it to Jake to learn a bit more before making his final decision.

After speaking with Jake for about half an hour, Randy learned what had led to Jake's misbehavior that day, and he gained a better understanding of the stress that he and his father had been going through for the past two years. Much of Jake's behavior, and that of his father's, was in response to a chain of unfortunate incidents that had occurred in their family. Over a two-year period, Jake's brother had died in a car accident, his father lost the job he'd had for 15 years, and Jake's mother and father had gone through a lengthy and bitter separation and divorce. Adding to the situation was the fact that, following the divorce, Jake's mother moved to a different part of the country. Each of these events had a strong effect on Jake's emotional state, and they created tremendous stress between Jake and his father. The anger and sadness that Jake was feeling led to his misbehavior. It was his way of showing his feelings and, in a way, crying for help.

Jake's father was doing the best he could to make a new life for Jake and himself. However, with the added stress of phone calls from the school, Jake's father had often run out of patience by the time he made it to the school. Jake's behavior, and his father's reactions, were the result of a huge accumulation of stress. Jake's father turned out to be a great father who just needed a bit more support getting back on track, and Jake just needed someone to listen to him. Jake accepted that he would have a consequence for his misbehavior, but he also recognized that many of his actions were the result of feelings that built up over time and needed to be resolved, and that they often had little to do with what was happening at school. Despite the many forces that influenced Randy's decision, he believes that he managed to sort through this complicated case and come to a solution that best helped this student.

FORCES AFFECTING THE SITUATION

Several forces affected the way Randy could deal with Jake. One of the strongest forces was Randy's concern for Jake's well-being. His decision could make things better for Jake, but it could also change his life forever. Randy had to carefully consider any decision he made. His decision was made all the harder because of his lack of confidence and his lack of experience in teaching. This was Randy's first year of teaching, so he did not have any experience upon which to draw when trying to decide the most appropriate course of action. Randy wondered if he had been misreading the signs of possible physical abuse. He consulted with other teachers and the administrator, but none of them seemed concerned; they had been dealing with this family for several years. Another strong force affecting Randy's decision was the pressure to report all suspicions of abuse to CPS. This is the law. Teachers are not supposed to question or investigate. They are supposed to report. Randy knows that if teachers fail to report a case and it turns out to be real, the police can bring charges against them. This reality weighed heavily on Randy's mind as he struggled to decide what was best for Jake.

The final force that affected Randy's decision was the pressure that came from the rest of the school community. Many of the other students and families were affected by, and concerned about, the behaviors Jake was exhibiting. If the consequences for misbehavior were not consistent, then Randy and his colleagues could lose parental support, and student behavior could become harder to manage.

CONCLUSION

Randy says he realized that when dealing with the multi-dimensional issues that arise in schools, the solution is rarely black and white. Though there were many forces that he believes pressured him to quickly resolve the issue with Jake, the best decision turned out to be compassion and understanding, rather than blind adherence to discipline policies.

REFLECTION AND DISCUSSION QUESTIONS: PRACTICAL AND PROFESSIONAL ETHICS

1. The law clearly states that teachers must report any suspicions of child abuse or neglect to either the police or to Child Protective Services (CPS). Randy did not do this. He did say, however, that he consulted with other teachers and the administrator, but none of them seemed concerned; they had been dealing with this family for several years. Do you think this qualifies as reporting the situation? Do you think this excuses him from following the law and reporting his suspicions to CPS?
2. If Randy justifies his actions by asking himself if specific policies address the emotional needs of a particular student, doesn't that open the door to question all policies for all students?
3. What might Kant say about situation-specific questioning and implementation of policy?
4. What might Mill or Plato say about situation-specific questioning and implementation of policy?
5. Randy clearly states that he knows that teachers are not supposed to investigate matters like this. Do you think what Randy did constitutes investigating this situation? Did Randy violate that policy?
6. Did Randy follow the law or did he break the law?

7. Was Jake better served, or was he harmed, by the way Randy handled this situation?
8. How would you handle this situation?

REFLECTION AND DISCUSSION QUESTIONS: DIFFERENTIATION OF SELF

1. Randy says many of the other students and families were affected by, and concerned about, the behaviors Jake was exhibiting, and if the consequences for misbehavior were not consistent, Randy and his colleagues could lose parental support, and student behavior could become harder to manage. Is the possibility of losing parent support a healthy motivation for decision making? If so, how do you decide which parents to listen to? If not, what kind of parent or community feedback guides your decision making?
2. Randy says Jake's father turned out to be a great father who just needed a bit more support getting back on track, and that Jake just needed someone to listen to him. Is empathy for situations like this a healthy motivation for decision making? If so, how might you be equally responsive to the multitude of family situations in schools? If not, how do you attend to the emotional reality of students' lives?

15

Native Status, Politics, and the Hiring Process

I've wondered if my status as an enrolled member of a local tribe was why I was hired. I hope it's not, but I suspect it was. I think it was a political move on the part of the superintendent.

Sheila

Several years ago, Sheila Lake was preparing for a job interview for a teaching position in a small, rural school. Sheila had worked in this district as a summer maintenance worker. For that job, she had faced a panel of three interviewers, so she was prepared for a more in-depth interview process for the teaching position. Sheila says she experienced several days of gut-wrenching scenarios playing out in her mind about what was going to happen during the interview. The most gut-wrenching scenario consisted of a panel of principals, teachers, parents, and the superintendent asking her difficult questions about child development, curriculum, classroom management, assessment and evaluation of student progress—all of which she would be unable to answer.

At the time of the interview, Sheila walked into the boardroom. She saw the superintendent alone, sitting at the head of the table, drinking coffee. There was a file in front of him. His demeanor was casual, which helped Sheila relax somewhat. The superintendent asked Sheila some questions about the school and about working with the maintenance department. As Sheila waited for other board members to join them and for the interview to begin, she became uncertain about what was going to happen. She thought that maybe she had made a mistake about the interview time, or that maybe she misunderstood and the position was not open anymore.

The superintendent opened the file and began to confirm Sheila's address, phone number, Social Security number, and the like. It was at that point that Sheila told the superintendent that she was confused, that she thought she was there for a job interview. The superintendent told Sheila there was no need for an interview, that she had the job and that he thought she realized that.

At first, Sheila was happy but slightly embarrassed that she had been so worried about the interview. After these emotions passed, she began to think about why she was given the position without an interview, without any competition, and without any references about her teaching ability. This is when Sheila began to wonder if she was hired because of who, or what, she is—Native American.

This is when her dilemma began. Should she question the matter and turn down the position, or should she be grateful and take the position. She took the position, telling herself that regardless of why she was hired, she would prove that she was a great teacher.

That particular school district was in the process of integrating the Native American Education Committee. There was a perceived need to have Native teachers working in the school system. Sheila understood this dynamic because there is a large Indian population in the schools in that area, and there is a shortage of Native teachers in the classrooms.

Sheila believes that, in theory, it is good practice to hire Native teachers to work with Native children, but she also believes that all teachers need to be qualified to fill these positions. Sheila, who had no experience other than her student teaching practicum, was being offered a job in a multi-grade school setting. Her student teaching practicum was in a single-grade classroom, and it did not prepare her for the task she was taking on. Yet, here she was, being hired without an interview for a complex teaching situation, with a hint of political overtones.

SHEILA'S RESPONSE

After taking the position, Sheila thought that maybe she was just being too sensitive about the process. She proceeded to take on the task of teaching three grade levels in one classroom. She used whatever resources were available, and she asked for help when she needed it because she knew she wanted to do the best job possible for the range of children in her class.

Sheila says she felt that she needed to prove to everyone involved, the students, the parents, her colleagues, the principal, and to herself, that she could be a good teacher. Sheila says that it actually took her several years to realize that she could stop doubting herself about the job she was doing.

During those years, she taught several different grade levels in multi-grade classrooms. She also taught physical education, art, and technology, all of which have given her the confidence to know that she provides a good education to all of the children in her class. She has become able to take compliments from colleagues, principals, and friends about her qualities as a teacher; whereas, earlier in her career she would justify their compliments as their merely being nice or politically motivated. It was the doubt about how she was hired that kept her from accepting the simple compliments being offered by the people in her life.

There have been several times throughout her career that Sheila has wondered if she should have confronted the superintendent at the time of the interview and asked if her status as an enrolled member of a local tribe was the reason she was hired. She says she hopes that was not the reason she was given a position in a rural school with a large percentage of Native American students, but in reality she suspects it was and that it was a political move on the part of the superintendent.

Would she have turned down the position? She says not. She would like to have thought that she would have been strong enough to stand up and say this is not the way she wants to be hired for an important position such as teaching. Sheila believes that she has justified herself by proving she is a good teacher. Not once has she ever shared these feelings with anyone, maybe out of shame, maybe because she knew they would disagree. Either way, Sheila had to prove herself.

Regardless of her heritage, Sheila has proven to herself that whatever the board's reason for hiring her, she has served her students and her community well. She was given the opportunity to prove that she could be a leader in the school. Her principal has met with her to express his appreciation about how she handled situations while he was away. The principal also told Sheila that she would be a good principal because she had the strength and determination to be fair to everyone.

Sheila believes that all teachers should be given a fair chance at new positions. She hopes that the practice of hiring or not hiring because of ethnicity has stopped. She may never know why she was hired because confirming her suspicions will not benefit anyone.

REFLECTION AND DISCUSSION QUESTIONS: PRACTICAL AND PROFESSIONAL ETHICS

1. Do beginning teachers have an ethical obligation to call attention to what they perceive to be questionable procedures?
2. Does a new teacher's going along with a questionable hiring procedure make her complicit in an ethically compromised situation?

3. Is proving oneself justification enough for taking a teaching position under questionable or politically motivated conditions?
4. Could the lack of process in this case be justified by an assumption of the superintendent's knowledge of Sheila's capabilities?
5. All qualifications being equal, can you make an ethical case for hiring Native teachers over non-Native teachers for Native American children on reservations, in rural areas, urban areas, suburban areas, and inner-city areas?
6. Draw upon the ethical theories to make a case that the superintendent, in not convening a full, formal review and hiring process, caused harm to Sheila Lake.

REFLECTION AND DISCUSSION QUESTIONS: DIFFERENTIATION OF SELF

1. Explain why you would, or would not, ever take a teaching position under the same conditions Sheila took this one.
2. Family systems theory views the family as an emotional unit, not just as a collection of individuals. It identifies the sources of physical, emotional, and social issues in the family or, in our case, schools. Sheila says she felt that as a result of the way she was hired, she needed to prove to everyone, including herself, that she could be a good teacher. She says it took several years for her to realize she could stop doubting herself. Sheila says she is now able to accept compliments about her qualities as a teacher; whereas, earlier she would justify their compliments as their merely being nice or politically motivated. She says it was the doubt about how she was hired that kept her from accepting compliments. Have you ever experienced such doubt about your abilities? If so, describe how it developed, where it came from, how you have dealt with it, and what the status of it is now.
3. What kinds of similarities can you see between families and schools in Sheila's situation?
4 What kinds of similarities can you see between family dynamics and school-based dynamics in your own experiences?

16

Being Used or Being of Service

My greatest fault is that I did not speak up and share my concerns. I was scared of the challenge. Not speaking up caused me to question whether or not my students were at the heart of my decision making.

Ms. Perkins

"As I think more about the demands of the teaching profession and as my perception of ethics and values begins to take shape, I question whether or not I am an 'ethical' teacher. As a teacher, I have acquainted myself with the ethics of my profession; however, I can't help but think of how much stronger my ethics could be if I understood them at a deeper level. I believe that, as teachers, we know about ethics, but we know in different ways. Ethics is about human values, aspiring toward higher standards, and operating with good will. The function of the code of ethics is to have standards about human value. When I look at teachers' codes of professional ethics, I see them acting as external forces that will encourage, support, and foster my values" (Ms. Perkins).

THE SITUATION

Ms. Perkins has been a first-grade teacher for four years. She says it has been a challenging, yet rewarding, experience for her. It has been challenging in the sense that her students are dependent in so many ways and, in many cases, their parents exude the same dependent tendencies, in that they require a lot of scheduled time with her.

Ms. Perkins has worked in a middle- to upper-social economic area for the past three years. She has been blessed with smaller class sizes and with few children with learning disabilities. At the beginning of the past year, the school had only enough students enrolled in first grade to run a single first-grade classroom, in addition to a single first/second-grade combination classroom. With the reduced first-grade student population, the school was left with some interesting decisions to make about how to place which students in what classes. The school had one first-grade child who had multiple learning disabilities. But, perhaps a greater challenge, due to their reputation, was the parents' needs. Another student in the class had some communication disabilities, and another student who had been held back in kindergarten would now be attending half-time kindergarten classes and half-time, first-grade classes.

However, these were only the children with identified needs. There were many children with behavioral issues that had to be recognized and placed as well. For a primary grade, the class sizes were quite high, with 27 students. The principal of the school had the final decision about how these children would be placed into classrooms, and Ms. Perkins believes that the principal distributed the students unfairly, due to the fact that she was given the majority of the students with exceptional needs.

In Ms. Perkins' school, the combination classroom had always held the prestigious image of being where the brighter, more independent children were placed, due to the nature of the dual curriculum. Unfortunately, this characterization had not changed with the current student population in the school. Rather than looking at the needs of the entire group of children, the strengths of various teachers, and looking at all possible combinations, the criteria for filling the combination classroom for the current year remained the same: it was reserved for the brighter, more independent children. These criteria left the teacher who taught the first/second-grade combination classroom in a wonderful position. These criteria, however, resulted in the regular first-grade classroom being filled with all of the special needs children and behavioral needs children. These criteria also resulted in the first-grade classroom teacher being handed a variety of high-maintenance parents. Ms. Perkins was assigned the regular first-grade class. She reports that knowledge of this placement kept her awake at night for weeks before school even started.

MS. PERKINS' EMOTIONAL RESPONSE

Ms. Perkins' initial gut response was that this was going to be a daunting school year. She knows that teachers assume the responsibility for teaching each and every student in their classrooms; however, this was going to be extremely challenging due to the increased number of students with special needs. Ms. Perkins' ideals are that each and every day she enters the classroom ready to help her students be successful. Her immediate task is to determine what strategies will help them succeed. Her situation requires an open mind, an understanding of what learning disabilities really are, and a willingness to accept the challenge of teaching students who have learning disabilities.

Mrs. Wilder, the teacher of the first/second-grade combination room, had been a teacher for 15 years. She made it clear that she would not be teaching the straight first-grade class. She said there were certain families that she did not care to work with because of knowing, from older siblings, the nature of these parents. She also stated that she did not think she could deal with the various Individualized Education Programs (IEPs) of all the children with special needs because she had been teaching the first/second-grade combination class for so long and she was used to working with the brighter, more independent children. Her assumption seemed to be that, because Ms. Perkins was younger and more open-minded, she would be more able to take on the challenges of this class.

Ms. Perkins wondered: Wouldn't the teacher with the most experience be more suitable for this challenging position? Ms. Perkins was not sure whether to feel flattered because her principal believed that she was capable of the task or feel taken advantage of because of all of the special needs students being placed in just one classroom—hers.

MS. PERKINS' INTELLECTUAL RESPONSE

Ms. Perkins did not feel she was trained well enough for that particular class. She believed current educational training programs make an unfortunate distinction between regular educators and special educators. This distinction lead her to the belief that there is some magical formula or skill that only the special educator possesses, but it also contributed to her feelings of being inadequately skilled to teach special needs students. She learned quickly that while those educators who have trained to work with students with special needs have studied extensively and possessed many skills for special needs instruction, the lessons they have learned actually originated with regular education teachers. After she saw that there were not going to be any changes in the two first-grade class lists, she started to embrace the challenge. She acknowledges that her growth as a teacher has been incredible, and she is aware of how much more she has to learn about working with special needs students.

Ms. Perkins says that the first month of working with her class of first graders was exhausting. She saw how the dynamics of her classroom were going to change how she taught. Her principal was supportive of her efforts. Some of her students' parents wanted to meet with her for an hour after school every week for the first month. At the end of the teaching day, this became draining. Mrs. Wilder would often make remarks to her such as, "I do not know how you do it" or "I could not teach that class."

Ms. Perkins says that after a while, she realized that in all fairness to the students, perhaps it was better, for two reasons, that these children were placed in her class. First, Mrs. Wilder had no desire to work with children with IEPs. Ms. Perkins now believes teachers must have an accurate understanding of learning disabilities and be open-minded in accepting and understanding a diagnosis of learning disabilities. Second, Mrs. Wilder had taught the combination classroom for so long that she had not changed her program in many years. She refused to do any team planning because she had her program set up and saw no need for changing it. Ms. Perkins now sees that teachers must accept the challenges of helping learning-disabled students succeed. To accomplish this, teachers must be willing to question their own teaching styles and techniques, be willing to attempt different strategies, and be creative and positive in working with parents. Ms. Perkins says that each day she learns something new about her students. What she saw before as a problem, she now sees as an opportunity.

FORCES AFFECTING THE SITUATION

Despite the positive outcome, Ms. Perkins says she felt very much alone in her situation. She approached Mrs. Wilder about planning together, but she always got a negative response. She wishes her principal would have stepped in and encouraged the two of them to team-plan as part of a school initiative. She believes the school needed to cultivate the awareness that we are all in this together and that consideration of each other is essential. Ms. Perkins believes that traditions play too strong of a role in the school, especially in assigning students to specific teachers and classrooms. She thinks that if Mrs. Wilder could have some experience in working with special needs children, she would not be so intimidated and insistent that working with them was something she didn't ever want to do. Do combination classes always have to be filled with the brightest and most independent students? As much as she grew from the experience, Ms. Perkins believes that educational professionals have to base their actions on what is best for students, not teachers.

CONCLUSION

Ms. Perkins says that her greatest fault in this situation was that she did not speak up and share her concerns with her principal about the distribution of students. She says she was scared of the challenge, but that she did not want her concerns to come across as her being unsure of her teaching abilities. In her estimation, not speaking up to her principal caused her to question whether her students were at the heart of her decision making.

Ms. Perkins says the experience has taught her that she needs to approach the challenges of the teaching profession with a thorough and accurate understanding of the students' needs and an enthusiastic attitude. She says professional ethics are about human values, aspiring toward higher standards, and about operating with good will. Quoting Gandhi, she said, "The best way to find yourself is to lose yourself in the service of others." She summarizes her new learning by saying, "If we remember to keep our students at the heart of our ethical decision making, we will be showing a higher standard of leadership."

REFLECTION AND DISCUSSION QUESTIONS: PRACTICAL AND PROFESSIONAL ETHICS

1. Even though the situation turned out well, what do you think about Ms. Perkins' criticisms aimed at the process used in placing the students?
2. Placing yourself in the position of the principal, draw upon at least two theorists to explain why you would or would not have placed any of the special needs students with Mrs. Wilder.
3. Placing yourself in the position of the principal, draw upon two different theorists to explain why you would or would not have placed the more experienced teacher in the regular first grade classroom with most of the special needs students.

REFLECTION AND DISCUSSION QUESTIONS: DIFFERENTIATION OF SELF

1. What do you think of the general claim made by Ms. Perkins that the more senior teachers seem to get their way? If it is true, do you think it is fair?
2. Ms. Perkins makes the claim that Mrs. Wilder preferred to not work with specific families or parents. Under what conditions do you think that might be a fair and legitimate request?

3. Do you think it is possible that when one person refuses to perform certain functions, others will—or have to? By refusing to work with certain kinds of children, what effect is Mrs. Wilder having on the school as a system?

4. Family systems theory sees physical, emotional, and social problems as part of a *relationship* process, not as cause and effect dynamics. What role does Ms. Perkins seem to be taking on in her relationship with Mrs. Wilder in this system?

5. What kinds of similarities, if any, can you see between this situation and the family in which you were raised?

6. What kinds of similarities, if any, do you see between the way you act and interact in your professional life and the family in which you were raised?

17

Bullies and Conflict with the School Principal

I felt guilty and frustrated for not doing enough for the victim. I felt that I was ethically compromised and that the bullies got away with their brutality.

Mr. Nestor

Mr. Nestor was in his second year of teaching sixth grade at St. Michael's Elementary School. Mr. Nestor had a student by the name of John McKenzie. John struggled with an array of learning disabilities that affected him academically. His learning disabilities also created problems for his ability to socialize with others, yet John was a kind and trusting individual who tried his best to fit in. His mother died when he was in third grade, and his dad was not very involved with him or his problems at school.

THE SITUATION

Mr. Nestor was in a staff meeting at the end of the day. The students had been dismissed, the playground was empty of kids, the busses had completed their runs, and all seemed well. The teachers finished the staff meeting and Mr. Nestor went home. The next morning, John went to Mr. Nestor before class and told him three students from St. Michael's peed on his stuff. Mr. Nestor took John aside and talked with him one-on-one to get all the details. This is the story John told Mr. Nestor: "Yesterday, at about 3:30, Art, Butch, and Craig cornered me behind the school and said they would beat me up if I didn't give them my money. I said no. They punched me and kicked me. They took my knapsack and ripped it open. They found my wallet and took $5.00 out of it. I thought it was all over, but then Art peed all over my knapsack and all my stuff. They went to the store and used my money to buy Slurpees for themselves." Mr. Nestor thanked John for telling him about the situation. He promised John that he would deal with it and that these boys would not get away with this.

MR. NESTOR'S EMOTIONAL RESPONSE

Mr. Nestor's initial response was one of anger. He felt sick about the fact that John had been violated in such a malicious and organized fashion. It was contradictory to the whole Catholic school philosophy and what teachers and administrators were trying to teach their students. Mr. Nestor wanted these three bullies to be punished for what they had done.

Mr. Nestor also felt a deep concern for John and how he was coping. Mr. Nestor wanted to be compassionate and show him empathy. John needed to know that Mr. Nestor was there for him and supported him. He said he needed to step back, analyze, and come up with a proactive approach for dealing with the situation.

MR. NESTOR'S INTELLECTUAL RESPONSE

After getting his emotional response under control, Mr. Nestor said that he began to think about what the best course of action might be. He needed to consider all of the people involved and what was in the best interest of John, the three bullies, and the school.

Mr. Nestor thought John needed first to be reassured and comforted, and know that the situation was being dealt with. Mr. Nestor also wanted to reassure John that school was a safe place to be, and that he could be free of unnecessary worry while he was at school.

Mr. Nestor says he also thought the three bullies needed to learn an important lesson, and that the consequences for their actions should provide opportunities for their personal growth. Consequently, he believed that a two-day, out-of-school suspension and a three-day in-school suspension was in order for the three bullies. Mr. Nestor also believed that the three bullies should be responsible for replacing John's knapsack and repaying the money they took. A sincere apology to John was an obvious requirement.

By making the bullies more aware of the harm they caused, Mr. Nestor believed the school could begin to work on meaningful reflection and growth. Mr. Nestor believed that the school should reinforce the positive qualities of leadership and provide the bullies with opportunities to model them. In this way, he hoped that they would think of others before acting out. Mr. Nestor wanted to help them internalize the Golden Rule.

Mr. Nestor believed he had an ethical responsibility to John and to the bullies. He thought that from a school standpoint, teachers and administrators needed to make sure they sent a clear message about what the school deemed to be non-acceptable behavior. The school motto, "Is it the loving thing to do?" motivated Mr. Nestor to act. When Mr. Nestor acted, however, he was surprised by the reaction he received from the school principal.

MR. NESTOR'S ACTIONS

Mr. Nestor reported the incident that day to the school principal. The principal told Mr. Nestor he would deal with it. By the end of the next day, nothing had been done. Knowing that John's father was not going to pursue the issue, Mr. Nestor believed he was put into an ethical dilemma. Mr. Nestor wanted to see action, and yet he was told the situation was being taken care of.

Mr. Nestor felt ethically obligated to confront his principal and ask what was being done. When Mr. Nestor suggested what he would like to see happen, he was accused by the principal of overstepping his boundaries. His principal said, "I can't believe that as a second-year teacher you would have the nerve and the gall to come in here and tell me what you would like to see happen."

Mr. Nestor did not get the support he was hoping for, and he now felt that he had compromised his position at St. Michael's. He felt belittled and unheard. The final decision about the bullying was made at the end of the week. The result was that the three boys were given a one-day, out-of-school suspension, and the knapsack would be cleaned. Mr. Nestor said that finishing that year at St. Michael's was very difficult for him.

FORCES AFFECTING THE SITUATION

Mr. Nestor believes a number of forces were at work, all of which had a negative effect on the final decision the principal made. The forces Mr. Nestor sees at play are that the principal supported some parents more than he did students or teachers, and the three bullies' parents were large stakeholders in, and supporters of, the school. Mr. Nestor also believes that the fact that John's father was not capable of defending his son adequately was a factor. Added to this, Mr. Nestor has seen that the principal generally wanted to maintain the caring image of the Catholic school, but that he did not want to create waves in the community. Mr. Nestor believes these forces worked against John and favored the bullies.

After this situation was over, Mr. Nestor reported that he felt guilty and frustrated for not doing enough for the victim. After such a minor consequence was given to the bullies, Mr. Nestor had a choice to push for a stiffer consequence, or to sit back and accept the decision. Mr. Nestor felt that he was ethically compromised and that the bullies got away with their brutality.

REFLECTION AND DISCUSSION QUESTIONS: PRACTICAL AND PROFESSIONAL ETHICS

1. What do you think of the consequences given to the bullies?
2. What do you think of Mr. Nestor's motives and the consequences he had in mind for the bullies?
3. When specific policies, with specific consequences, are in place for specific problematic behaviors, do you think one's motive matters in carrying out the policy?
4. Given that differences of opinion among professionals is highly likely, what professional responsibilities do teachers and principals have, to prevent differences of opinion from turning into the type of conflict shown in this case?
5. Draw upon at least two of the theoretical perspectives to explain whether or not the principal has an obligation to explain to Mr. Nestor the decision-making process he used to arrive at his decision.

REFLECTION AND DISCUSSION QUESTIONS: DIFFERENTIATION OF SELF

1. After this situation was over, Mr. Nestor reported that he felt guilty and frustrated for not doing enough for the victim. What more could he have done?
2. Doing all one can do can still feel like not doing enough. Guilt and frustration are natural feelings, especially in such situations. How might you deal, how have you dealt, with similar feelings?

18

An Emotionally, Intellectually, and Spiritually Punishing Year

I felt trapped. I didn't stand up for what I believed to be true. I wasn't strong enough to take whatever consequences the principal was going to throw my way. I wanted to please the principal so that I could get a good evaluation. The reward for conformity is that everyone likes you but yourself.

Esther

Esther was a first-year assistant principal at an elementary school. She was trained as a secondary teacher, so this assignment meant that she was placed into a setting that was completely foreign to her. The administrative team at the school consisted of the principal and Esther. The principal and Esther did not get along. They did not have the same leadership styles, and Esther found it very difficult to follow her orders. The principal was highly autocratic and controlling. Esther's leadership style is more personable and friendly. Esther prefers to approach her coworkers as colleagues, as people she can talk to and get to know. The principal did not work well with others, and she would not listen to others or take any kind of feedback without getting very defensive. As a result of their differences, there were many examples Esther could share of ethically compromising positions. One of these situations, in particular, stands out for her.

THE SITUATION

The principal and Esther usually de-briefed at the end of each day. However, it had been a busy week and they had not discussed matters of the week for a couple of days. At the end of their meeting, Esther was sharing with the principal a few minor incidents that occurred with a couple of staff members. To Esther, the incidents were no big deal. The principal, however, wanted to know everything that was going on in the school. From Esther's previous experiences with the principal, Esther knew she would be upset with her if Esther forgot to tell her the slightest detail because the principal did not want to come across to others as not being informed of everything.

So, Esther mentioned that a few staff members had let their students out approximately three minutes early for lunch. The first incident happened when Esther was in the gym and a group of grade-two students came into the gym without a homeroom teacher. Esther approached the teacher and explained to her that it was not in her best interest to do that because there was no supervision in the gym for students who were dismissed early. Esther and the teacher talked about it, and the teacher promised not to do it again. Esther never gave this incident another thought. A few days later, another staff member dismissed her students early and Esther found them at their lockers and wandering the hallways. Esther sent the students back to class and talked to this staff member, reminding her that she should not dismiss her students before the bell. Again, the staff member understood Esther's position. As with the previous incident, Esther never gave it another thought.

Esther shared these stories with her principal. The principal was visibly upset that Esther did not deal with these matters more severely. Esther said that she believed that it did not need to be dealt with in any more severity. Esther told the principal that the staff members had agreed not to dismiss their students early, and Esther believed them. The principal then told Esther that she had had to deal with these two particular staff members before, for other reasons. For the principal, these incidents were not minor and required more disciplinary action. The principal wanted Esther to officially write them each a letter explaining the severity of dismissing students early from class, and stating that the next time they broke a school rule, a letter would be written and sent downtown to central office and placed in their personnel files.

ESTHER'S EMOTIONAL AND INTELLECTUAL RESPONSES

When the principal told Esther what she wanted her to do, Esther was furious with her. Esther's heart rate immediately shot up and so did her breathing. Esther wanted to scream at the principal for being so irrational. Esther did not believe that her decision had any merit. For Esther, this situation and her response to it were about trusting in the people she worked with and treating them with respect and dignity. They did not need to be treated as children. They did not need to be scolded. They were intelligent individuals who made a promise to Esther that they were not going to dismiss their students early. Esther believed in them.

Esther did not write the letter right away. She did not sleep well that night because she felt that she was being forced to do something that she did not want to do. Not only that, but Esther knew in her heart it was the wrong thing to do and that it would destroy, or at the very least, damage the relationships she had established with these two colleagues. Writing such a letter was not her style of leadership. Esther was not someone who scolded others or needed to control their actions in any way. She felt sick inside and her guts were in total knots. Esther believed that, because the principal felt so strongly about the incidents, she should be the one to write the letter.

Esther also felt trapped because she wanted to receive a good evaluation at the end of her year as an assistant principal at that school. This principal would be the person who would write Esther's evaluation, and they had already had their share of disagreements and arguments. Esther was getting very tired of constant conflict with the principal. Esther was also getting tired of being bullied and pushed around. However, she did not know how to stop the bullying. She had already met with the superintendent two times, and he was aware of Esther's and the principal's professional and personal differences and struggles. Esther was doing the best she could in a bad situation.

ESTHER'S ACTIONS

The following day, Esther arrived at the school determined to tell the principal that she would not write this letter. Esther was going to explain to the principal that she did not feel comfortable in writing a letter that, to her, had no merit. Esther was still shaky and nervous about having to write this letter.

When the principal came into the school that morning, Esther went to see her right away. Esther told the principal that she did not feel comfortable in writing a letter that the principal felt more strongly about. Esther suggested that if the principal felt the situations were so severe, that the principal should write the letters. The principal did not like Esther's response.

Later, the principal went into Esther's office and closed the door. She explained to Esther that there were times as an administrator that Esther would have to do things she did not feel comfortable doing. Esther believed this to be true; however, in her own thinking, she did not believe that this situation was worthy of further reprimands or discussion. According to the principal, this situation was severe enough to warrant a letter. The principal told Esther that she, Esther, was going to write those letters and when she did, she was to make sure she carbon copied the principal's name on the bottom of the letters so the staff members would know that the principal knew of the situation. The principal told Esther that if she did not write the letters, that the principal would have to consider a formal consequence for Esther, due to her lack of cooperation.

Esther's guts went raw. She really hated the principal in that moment, yet she felt powerless to do anything about it. Esther ended up calling a friend of hers who was also a principal within the same school district. Esther asked him for some advice. Esther told him that she felt cornered into a position in which there was no easy way out. He was very helpful. He gave Esther some professionally astute advice. He told Esther to write the letters, but to do so in such a way that the letter minimized the incident and in language that was more suited to her personality. So that is what Esther did. Her letters to these staff members were two sentences long. They were brief and succinct.

Esther cringed when she placed the letters in their mailboxes in the staff room. She felt sick and trapped. Of course, the staff members reacted negatively to these letters. One staff member confided in Esther that they could not believe that she wrote these letters. They felt it was so unlike her. Esther wished they could know the stress, grief, and trouble she went through in having to write those letters.

From that point on, Esther's relationship with those staff members changed. They were cold and distant toward her and did not talk to her on a friendly level for the rest of the school year. It broke Esther's heart. She ended up being very angry with herself for not being stronger with the principal. However, she was not in a place in her life where she felt she could be stronger. It had been a punishing year emotionally, intellectually, and spiritually.

FORCES AFFECTING THE SITUATION

Esther believes that the obvious main force that affected the situation was the principal; the principal was the bully and Esther was the victim, and that she did not stand up for what she believed to be true, for her. She was not strong enough to take whatever consequences the principal was going to throw Esther's way. Esther wanted to please the principal so that she could get a good evaluation and transfer out of that school. This leads to the second force that affected the situation: Esther's evaluation.

Esther was so concerned about her evaluation that she did what she was told to do. Esther was living in a sea of fear. She was so fearful of what the principal was going to write about her that she rolled over and did as she was told. She did not have clear personal boundaries and she did not stand up for herself.

Another force that Esther believes affected the situation was the fact that Esther was doing her best to remain professional in her relationship with the principal. She did not want other staff members to know how she really felt about the principal or that the principal and Esther did not get along. Esther wanted everyone to think everything was okay.

The final force for Esther was doing her best not to get angry. She ended up biting her lip so many times that she felt like a cannon about to go off. So, in the times when she disagreed with the principal, instead of getting in an argument, Esther would comply with the principal's requests. At the same time, she felt that at any moment she was going to tell the principal off, but then she, Esther, would look like the one who was completely irrational.

Maintaining a professional relationship with someone with whom she did not share a common leadership style or philosophy and who treated others with disrespect, has been the most challenging experience of Esther's professional life so far. She will never forget this experience and the lessons it taught her.

REFLECTION AND DISCUSSION QUESTIONS:
PRACTICAL AND PROFESSIONAL ETHICS

1. Esther and the principal had strong differences of opinion regarding the issue described in this case. The principal claimed to have prior similar experiences with these teachers. Given that claim, what do you think of the principal's administrative response of insisting that letters be sent to these teachers?
2. Esther said she had previously met with the superintendent two times and he was already aware of Esther's and the principal's professional and personal differences and struggles. What do you think of the ethics of Esther's actions in going to visit with the superintendent about the issues between Esther and the principal?
3. How might Rand have handled the situation?
4. If you aspire to be a school administrator, what kinds of personal and professional issues do you see in Esther's case that might be worth thinking about?

REFLECTION AND DISCUSSION QUESTIONS:
DIFFERENTIATION OF SELF

1. Have you ever complied with a superior's wishes in order to get a good evaluation? If so, how did that feel? What are the ways in which you benefited or suffered?

2. How long would you put up with something at work that was emotionally, intellectually, and spiritually punishing?
3. Describe a situation in which you did not put up with something that was so punishing.
4. Describe a situation in which you did put up with, or still are putting up with, something that was, or is, so difficult.

19

An Exercise in Common Sense

I tolerated what I should have challenged; I hesitated when I should have
spoken.

Doug

Ethical practice, in some respects, can be the exercise of common sense. On
occasion, the decisions of colleagues might appear unethical because they
defy common sense. Or, at least, they defy one's own common sense.
Therein lies the conflict of ethics and the potential for compromise.

THE SITUATION

One morning in November, as Doug was walking through the school, he
caught sight of a little boy through the window of a teacher's office. In
Doug's school, the teachers' offices are adjacent to their rooms, and two
teachers share one office. The design of the rooms has the office jut out like
a bay window into the hallway, so one can peer into an office without dis-
turbing a classroom.

The child Doug saw was sitting on an office chair, playing at the computer. The little boy's name was Jason; Doug recognized him as the son of
a couple of teachers on staff. Jason is a delightful five-year-old with a quick
smile and a sweet charm, but what was Jason doing here, at school, in the
middle of the morning?

A glance into the class to the left of the office revealed that Jason's dad
was teaching; a glance into the class to the right of the office revealed that

Jason's mom was teaching, also. Jason was happily surfing one of his favorite websites, his parents were busy teaching, and there was no immediate concern, so Doug kept walking past the window.

Doug made a mental note of Jason's presence and chalked it up to some
unforeseen circumstance that left Jason's parents with little choice but to
tuck him into the office until they finished their lessons for the morning.
Three days later, Doug noted the second occasion of Jason's presence in his
parents' office during class time.

Jason is registered in Kindergarten at this school, but he is an afternoon
student. Jason's father is a full-time teacher, but his mother is teaching only
part-time. Several mornings a week, Jason's mother is required to be at
school for only one hour. It became apparent that Jason's parents were
bringing him to school instead of placing him in daycare for that hour. A
quick examination of the parents' teaching schedules suggested that this
pattern would surface on Mondays, Wednesdays, and Fridays, and that went
on for the months of November, December, and January. For three months,
Doug continued to walk past and say nothing. All the while, Doug struggled
with his own indecision about the inappropriateness of his colleagues' actions.

DOUG'S EMOTIONAL RESPONSE

Doug says that he was in emotional conflict about this situation. He could
empathize with this family in a very direct fashion because he, too, has
young children. Furthermore, in the early autumn, he had overheard these
parents' comments about how much Jason disliked daycare. Doug has also
experienced the displeasure of trying to drop his daughter off at daycare and
all the while she was crying to not be left behind. That experience created a
difficult morning and a painful memory, to say the least.

Doug says he caught himself rationalizing in favor of Jason's parents. For
example, what harm did it really do to have Jason play on a computer in the
office? It was only for an hour or so at a time. His parents were just on the
other side of the office door. Jason was not bothering anyone. Besides,
didn't our school welcome children into the building at the end of the
school day? Other teachers had their children meet them in our building at
the end of the day. Given that the school day ends at 3:30, these children
usually arrived while classes were still in session. These other children
waited for their parents in the offices adjacent to their own parents' classrooms. In fact, Doug's own daughter has met him at school on occasion. So
did the principal's children. Were Jason's morning visits at school during
classes really any different?

Doug says he was also moved by a sense of sympathy toward Jason's parents because they have had their share of "attention" from the office in the

last two years. Each parent has had his or her conduct called into question. Evaluations, reprimands, and discipline letters have characterized the relationships between the parents and the principal at the school. Jason's parents perceived Doug to be the last person on staff with whom they had a positive working relationship; Doug says he was, therefore, reluctant to jeopardize that, more for their sakes than his own. As the weeks passed, Doug maintained a hope that Jason's parents would come to see the error in their judgment without his intervention. This irrational hope drove the rational, unsympathetic part of him crazy!

DOUG'S INTELLECTUAL RESPONSE

Doug now believes that the situation was actually black and white: Children do not accompany their parents to work. Wouldn't common sense dictate such a conclusion? Of course, it would. People are not able to do their jobs fully and completely if their own child is sitting unsupervised nearby. Doug knew that he couldn't do his work if his child was there with him, and he could not fathom the thinking of a parent who would insist otherwise. Thinking that someone must have written a specific policy prohibiting such a practice, he searched the Manual of School Law, the District Policy Manual, and the Staff Handbook. Doug could find nothing specific about anything like this.

Then Doug realized: Of course there were no policies governing such behavior! Reasonable people do not need to be directed to leave their children at home. Reasonable people understand that their work will suffer if a child that needs to be supervised distracts them. A reasonable teacher certainly understands that supervising 30 children belonging to someone else is demanding enough without including one's own child who happens to be five years old and in an adjoining office! Doug says that the rational part of his decision making resented the need to address such an issue with a teacher; it seemed ridiculous.

Doug further resented the fact that, because he was an administrative intern training to be a principal, the task of addressing the issue was now being delegated to him. He believed that such an intervention was the domain of a more senior administrator, namely, the principal. Doug was not the principal nor was he earning the principal's salary. A petty thought, perhaps, but truthfully one that affected his actions.

Deepening this resentment was Doug's own sense of duty: He believed that he should be able to do hard things, that he must meet the challenge of intervening with his two colleagues' use of the school as daycare. Doug's self-criticism and his fear of failure as an administrative intern hardened his resentment toward the situation and the principal. As Doug put it, "Damn my principal for making me feel this way!"

January came to an end, as did the situation: Jason did not show up for a week. Without any intervention on his part, without any effort toward a resolution, Doug's problem appeared to be solved. This relief was short lived. Jason returned in the following week, the first week of a new semester. His parents' schedules revealed that Jason would be "attending class" every Tuesday and Wednesday. The parents were going to continue to bring Jason to school; why wouldn't they? No one had told them not to.

DOUG'S ACTIONS

Doug realized that the situation had to be dealt with now, before more weeks passed and he spent another minute agonizing over this issue. He resolved to meet with Jason's parents at the end of the day on that first Tuesday of the new semester.

Doug said that he tried to arm himself with subterfuge before the meeting: "I researched the issue with the Workers' Compensation Board. I wanted something on which to hang my insistence that Jason be placed in daycare. I wanted some law, rule, or policy that could be responsible for this bureaucratic insensitivity. I found no such shelter. I would have to meet the parents unshielded and be responsible for calling them on their unprofessional practice. The bell rang at 3:30, and I headed to their shared office."

In respect to the ethical compromise Doug had been enduring, the details of the meeting are as revealing as they are anticlimactic. As soon as Doug began walking toward his colleagues' office that day, the hardest step had been taken; he had overcome his dilemma of whether or how to address the situation. He hardly had to utter more than the boy's name before Jason's father said, "Yeah, I know. I've never been really comfortable with this whole situation." That was it. Without much more said, the meeting was over. While Doug felt a great deal of relief, he was surprised at the apparent relief he observed in Jason's father. It would seem that he had not been the only one struggling with the ethics of the situation.

As Doug now frames it, "Perhaps a small town has a role to play in this ethical compromise. We live in each others' pockets in this town; our colleagues are also our friends. This familiarity breeds tolerance and hesitance. I tolerated what I should have challenged, and I hesitated when I should have spoken. In reflection, the delay was probably more damaging than the poor judgment exercised by Jason's parents. My failure to act left all parties in a state of limbo. The situation dragged on for months, and it was beginning to involve more staff. Others were confronted by their own sense of ethical compromise as they complained to me about Jason's parents. My discussing the issue with Jason's mom and dad in November would have, itself, been an exercise in common sense. A reasonable person has come to understand that."

REFLECTION AND DISCUSSION QUESTIONS: PRACTICAL AND PROFESSIONAL ETHICS

1. Explain whether or not you think Jason's parents were out of line in using the teachers' office and computer as their own in-house day care.
2. Explain whether or not you think the principal was justified in asking a principal-in training to handle this situation.
3. Do teachers have an ethical obligation to call attention to their colleagues' behaviors, such as this, that they might find to be questionable? If so, to whom? If not, why not?
4. Do principals-in-training have a right, or an obligation, to say what requests from the principal might be beyond their skill level or comfort level?
5. Even though this situation worked out fairly well, if a principal-in-training were to go along with a questionable request from a principal, which one of them would be responsible for a negative outcome?
6. Even though this issue was a matter of common sense, Doug tried hard to find a specific rule, law, or policy to support him when he addressed the issue with Jason's parents. He did not find any. What does this suggest to you?

REFLECTION AND DISCUSSION QUESTIONS: DIFFERENTIATION OF SELF

1. What are the similarities and differences between the phrase, "Argue for your limitations and, sure enough, they're yours!" and expressing to a principal that something might be beyond your skill level or comfort level?
2. Bowen suggests that differentiation, which is "the degree to which people are able to distinguish between the feeling process and the intellectual process" (1978, p. 88), is key to being a successful family member. For our purposes, this differentiation of self, this ability to distinguish between the feeling process and the intellectual process, is one of the keys to effectively managing ethically complex situations. How do you think Doug did in distinguishing between the feeling process and the intellectual process in this situation?

20

Ducking and Weaving through a Course in Human Sexuality

> This feeling was foreign to me. Confusion was my overwhelming emotion. With 20/20 hindsight, the entire situation seems almost comical, for surely if I were to encounter a like situation today, I would go with my gut and teach the students, not the curriculum.
>
> Charlotte

"The year of my most profound professional growth occurred when, after teaching at the middle school level for five years, I transferred to a high school. The move was scintillating and petrifying at the same time, because I faced the daily challenges of finding my place among a staff that was four times larger than at my previous school. At the same time, I was tackling the curricular challenges of teaching five new courses in four separate content areas attached to four different departments" (Charlotte).

Thus, in a new environment and responsible for an unaccustomed course, Charlotte became ensnared in a troubling ethical dilemma. She was required to teach a course, Career, Life, and Social Skills (CLASS), that directly conflicted with her values as a teacher. In Charlotte's district, three credits in CLASS are required before a high school diploma is granted. In both the curriculum guide and the school handbook, this course was described as a "values-neutral" experience. Charlotte points out now, "The absurdity of the term is now lit up like fireworks in my brain, because everything from the spelling primer to *Don Quixote* contains values."

THE CURRICULUM AND THE STUDENTS

The CLASS curriculum was supposed to be values free, but there was one exception. The human sexuality unit, a mandatory component of the course, was based on the premise that sexual abstinence until marriage was the best option. Thus, when the sections on birth control, sexually transmitted diseases, and sexual orientation were taught, the over-reaching theme was supposed to be one of abstinence. The difficulty Charlotte ran into with this was that of the 34 students enrolled in her class, five were parenting at the time. It seemed to her that "these parenting students were engaged in a courageous and hopeful act in returning to school and overcoming challenges of child care and economics. The gay students in the room rubbed against the abstinence stance as well, for certainly, the idea of a legally sanctioned union in which the 'preferred' abstinence gave way to marriage was not an option at all for them."

Charlotte had spent five years as a middle schoolteacher in a high-needs school dominated by students struggling to master English as a second language, and she had come to realize that sometimes all a teacher can do is discourage, encourage, or rearrange the students' learning patterns. Faced with a high absentee and dropout rate, Charlotte had made a point of reading as many authors' books on at-risk learners as she could, and she swore that she "would always make her classroom welcoming and safe for all learners." Thus, to teach that abstinence was preferred, or right, would imply that her parenting students and their children were somehow less valued or wrong. And Charlotte knew that a child could not be made wrong and safe at the same time.

Around the same time, the CLASS curriculum was receiving a lot of negative press. At another local high school, some parents had taken to sitting in on one slice of their students' CLASS classes, perhaps hearing only the guest lecturer from Planned Parenthood. These parents were engaged in a battle and were using the press as their battlefield. Charlotte loathed the idea of making an error in judgment and ending up as a casualty in this war. Thus, as she says, her ethical dilemma was to go against her gut instinct and teach the curriculum as it was written, or to go against the law, that is, the legal curriculum, and remain as "value neutral" as she could.

CHARLOTTE'S EMOTIONAL RESPONSE

Because teaching is Charlotte's passion and because she believes that teachers must always teach from where the students are, she felt confused and conflicted in this dilemma. Part of the reason she received the coveted position of high schoolteacher was because of her reputation as a team player, one who could happily get the job done and help others do the same. Thus, she was afraid of making waves over the curriculum, because she thought *good team players just didn't do this*. Charlotte says that she has since learned that good team players *do* make waves at times; very skilled team players cast their waves in a manner that will help get the ship to the most desirable shore.

At the same time all this was going on, Charlotte learned that she was pregnant. As Charlotte puts it, "The joy and fear I felt helped me emphasize with my brave student-parents and the complexity of my emotions cast more shadows onto the waves of my journey." As the week for the sexuality unit crept up on her, she began to dread teaching the CLASS material. She said, "This feeling was foreign to me; since my earliest days as a teacher, I have always looked forward to learning with the students. I wished for early maternity leave, but I was less than three months pregnant. Confusion was my overwhelming emotion."

CHARLOTTE'S INTELLECTUAL RESPONSE

Charlotte has come to understand that the forces that shaped her intellectual response were predominantly due to being raised in a duty-culture family, where she was taught that people must sacrifice their desires and do as they are told by authority without questioning the process. The administrative team at the school seemed, at that time, distant to Charlotte. Later, she was to learn that they were impressed with her skills, approach, and attitude, and they desired to keep her at all costs (they eventually wrestled with the Teachers' Union over whether they could keep her on staff, ahead of more experienced teachers). At the time, Charlotte felt that she must do as her position demanded and teach the curriculum to the letter of the law.

CHARLOTTE'S ACTIONS

Because she was a new teacher in this school, trying to prove herself to her new colleagues, she did not want to appear to lack confidence, and thus she was hesitant to go to the CLASS curriculum leader with her dilemma. The other people teaching the course were mainly the ones who had it tacked onto their teaching loads; it seemed that the course that demanded the most sensitivity was the one in which no person was truly a specialist. Charlotte's new school was large enough that a whole week could go by and she would not see another CLASS teacher, let alone approach one for advice. And if she did talk to any of these teachers, she often found that they didn't find the course worth much consideration. One teacher actually passed students based on their merely showing up and not falling asleep. This was hardly the approach a passionate educator such as Charlotte could adopt.

"I was feeling bothered and sour, and thinking that I would just have to keep a stiff upper lip and get on with the distasteful task. I considered that it would be much like changing a baby: smelly and unpleasant, but necessary. Then, as often happens, the universe intervened." Charlotte's CLASS curriculum leader put a memo in her mailbox. The memo stated that anyone who was teaching CLASS for the first time could request support from the team members for the human sexuality unit. The team members would provide four sessions, with an optional fifth session on sexual orientation, to the class. This support was available just once per teacher to those who taught the CLASS curriculum.

Charlotte scheduled all of the sessions, including the one on sexual orientation. The instructor for these sessions was a young, vivacious woman with a sense of humor. She made the students feel at ease almost instantly. The program was based on the curriculum, but did not advocate for abstinence or for sexual activity. It was designed to empower students with information while affirming that each of them would make suitable decisions based on their own values and beliefs. Charlotte remained in the room, but, for all intents and purposes, the resource person became the teacher. Charlotte saw it as a win-win situation because all of the students were invited to learn, and she did not have to go against those good-worker-bee traits that she had grown up with and developed further in her career.

FORCES AFFECTING THE SITUATION

Many forces affected Charlotte's situation. At times, each one became a dominating force, depending on the day and her emotional and intellectual state. First, the prescribed curriculum was a force. Second, her belief that all students must be welcomed and encouraged to learn in a safe environment was a force. Another factor was her beginner's status at teaching in the high school; and attached to this was her perceived lack of a support network. Charlotte's desire to do an outstanding job and remain at the school, without making waves, was another factor. The fact that her administrative team seemed distant (although they would later prove to be very approachable and supportive) also figured in. The vociferous concerns of the parents increased the pressure of the situation. And, finally, Charlotte's own imminent entry into the state of parenthood was another factor.

CONCLUSION

Charlotte summarizes this learning episode in her career like this: "With my 20/20 hindsight, the entire situation now seems almost comical, for surely if I were to encounter a like situation today, I would go with my gut and teach the students, not the curriculum. But I cannot underestimate the realness and rawness of my emotions at that time, for if a person perceives a situation to be stressful, then it is so, and no one may rightly argue otherwise. In a way, I got to duck and weave a little bit. Perhaps this was not the right way to go, but I know I would have more fortitude now. Still, the students and the school both received what they needed. And, in this profession, if nobody cried, nobody died, and nobody bled, it was a good day indeed!"

REFLECTION AND DISCUSSION QUESTIONS: PRACTICAL AND PROFESSIONAL ETHICS

1. Draw upon at least two ethical perspectives to explain whether teachers have an ethical obligation to teach whatever curriculum the school, district, or state requires, even if the teachers find the content to be questionable, inaccurate, or offensive.
2. How might Rand and Gandhi talk about the very existence of the CLASS curriculum?
3. Charlotte states, "With my 20/20 hindsight, the entire situation now seems almost comical, for surely if I were to encounter a like situation today, I would go with my gut and teach the students, not the curriculum." What kind of ethical compromises might be created by Charlotte's "teaching the students, not the curriculum"?

REFLECTION AND DISCUSSION QUESTIONS: DIFFERENTIATION OF SELF

1. What might you do if you were to encounter a curriculum that is as much of an issue to you as the CLASS curriculum was to Charlotte?
2. What are your thoughts regarding the idea of a "values-free" curriculum?
3. Charlotte describes this experience as "the year of my most profound professional growth." Describe your most profound professional growth so far, and what made it so.

21

Mama Bear Ethics

Gandhi asks us to reject physical violence and violence to the spirit. Although I did not intentionally violate Mrs. Camden's spirit, and perhaps I actually violated my own, I regret that she experienced such emotional trauma. I will take ownership for my own actions, I will be truthful, and I will continue to pursue my ideals of higher standards of education and leadership.

Angela

In late September, a letter from the principal of Angela's son's school arrived home in his backpack. The principal wrote to tell Angela that, due to district-wide staffing procedures, Mrs. Baker, her son's second grade teacher, would regretfully be leaving at the end of the month and, beginning on the first of October, a teacher with greater seniority in the district would take her place. Angela was a teacher in the same district, so she understood this process.

As announced, Mrs. Baker left, Mrs. Camden arrived and the class carried on. Although Mrs. Baker and Mrs. Camden never met and they were never provided with common planning time or teaching time in the classroom, the transition from the one to the other seemed to go smoothly.

October and November passed. Angela's son, Christopher, continued to come home every day enthusiastic and happy about his time at school. At the end of November, Angela had the opportunity to visit Christopher's classroom for an afternoon. She was pleased with what she saw as a well-organized learning environment and a positive, student-centered climate. Mrs. Camden seemed to take genuine pleasure in the children. Angela felt positive about the potential for Christopher's second-grade year. Before leaving the classroom that afternoon, Angela thanked Mrs. Camden for sharing the afternoon with her, and she complimented Mrs. Camden on the wonderful learning climate she appeared to have established.

THE REPORT CARD

Angela's son loves school. He has always been an excited, self-initiating learner. Being the youngest of Angela's three children, he has had the advantage of many intentional and serendipitous teachings. At age four, Angela's son insisted on learning to read. At five, he embraced the structured learning environment of Kindergarten. At the age of six, he excelled in his work in first grade. His mediocre second-grade report card stopped Angela in her tracks.

Angela's school district, like many others, uses a qualitative, ordinal marking system. Grades are presented as "1" through "5", with "1" representing the highest mark. The report card of student progress is divided into two distinct areas of development. The child's affective development is measured in terms of personal growth, work habits, and student effort. In these areas, a "1" represents excellence, a "2" means very good, a "3" stands for satisfactory, a "4" shows a need for improvement, and a "5" indicates the behavior or skill is not yet developed. A child's academic development is assessed through skill and concept attainment in each of the various subject areas. In these subject areas, the "1" through "5" rankings parallel the behavioral indicators.

In addition, the reporting on academic achievement includes two descriptive sentences per grade, meant to differentiate between the five marks. The report card breaks each subject area into specific observable skills and is comprised of 43 performance indicators per reporting period. With three formal reporting periods, 129 performance indicators are given for the entire academic year. On his grade-one report card, Angela's son received a total of seven 3s throughout the entire year. Marks of 1s and 2s comprised the remaining 122 marks. On his first second-grade report card, Angela's son received 25 3s, a stark contrast from the previous year.

THE INITIAL INTERVIEW

Angela arrived early at the Parent/Teacher conference. She brought with her a small gift of bottled water and fresh fruit for Christopher's teacher. In order to participate in the scheduled interview times, Angela had to make special arrangements at the school where she taught.

After some initial small talk, Mrs. Camden asked Angela if she had any concerns or questions about the report card. When Angela told Mrs. Camden that she had many questions and deep concerns, Mrs. Camden's back straightened; she seemed completely caught off guard. Angela expressed her concern for the significant decrease in Christopher's academic progress and effort, the sharp contrast in his grades from last year, along with the discrepancy between the indicated effort at school and his effort and interest Angela observed at home.

Throughout the course of the 15-minute interview, Mrs. Camden failed to validate Angela's concerns. Instead, Mrs. Camden insisted that Angela's son was doing well and that she had no significant concerns regarding his behavior or learning. Mrs. Camden informed Angela that *none* of her students received any 1s. Mrs. Camden asked Angela if she thought a 3 was a bad mark, and informed Angela that the grades of 3s did not indicate problems. Angela explained to Mrs. Camden that she, Angela, was interpreting the 3s as defined by the school district. Angela then read the definition of a 3 directly from Christopher's report card. "A grade of '3' indicates satisfactory progress and indicates that the student is able to use and apply most skills and strategies." Angela reiterated the significant change from seven 3s in his entire grade-one year to 25 3s in just one reporting period. Angela explained that 25 3s indicated 25 distinct areas in which Christopher was not using or applying all skills or strategies.

When Angela asked Mrs. Camden to describe the specific skills and strategies Christopher was not using, Mrs. Camden was unable to articulate even one. Mrs. Camden appeared to tremble and avert her eyes. Angela expressed that, as a mother, she was deeply concerned about Christopher's progress and she would like to be as helpful as possible in his learning, especially at home. To do so, it was important for her to know, specifically, what skills required her attention and how she could best help Christopher improve his understanding and performance.

Mrs. Camden covered her mouth with her hand, looked down, and appeared to be crying. Angela sat, waiting for a response. After a period of silence, Angela tried to comfort Mrs. Camden. Angela again expressed her desire to help. Again, Mrs. Camden did not reply. Mrs. Camden looked up briefly at Angela and then returned her teary gaze to the table. Angela and Mrs. Camden sat quietly for some time. Angela asked Mrs. Camden if she could talk with Angela about Christopher's reading.

In the first grade, Angela's son received straight 1s in all areas of reading in every reporting period. In this grading period, the first one of second grade, he received 3s and one 2. Not getting any response, Angela thought that if she asked Mrs. Camden something more specific, Mrs. Camden could regain her composure and complete the Parent/Teacher interview. Angela then asked if Mrs. Camden could share the results of the reading tests with her. Mrs. Camden seemed grateful for the opportunity to get up from the table. She quickly went to the filing cabinet and shuffled through some papers. As she continued to search through her files, Angela began to wonder if Mrs. Camden had actually performed a reading assessment on Christopher. When Mrs. Camden produced one, Angela wondered if perhaps Mrs. Camden had been intentionally stalling, allowing time to collect herself.

When Mrs. Camden returned to the interview table, she appeared to be shaking, flustered, and unable to clearly explain the results of the diagnostic reading test she had administered in early October. She interpreted the results three different ways, quickly correcting herself each time she read them. Angela was not clear about the results, and she thought it was best if she left that issue alone for now, too. It was clear to Angela at this point that Mrs. Camden had little understanding of Christopher as a student, how he learned best, what support he needed, or what areas of strengths he had. Mrs. Camden was now visibly crying. The scheduled appointment time ended. Angela suggested that she and Mrs. Camden meet again, at a later date, to complete the Parent/Teacher interview. Through teary eyes, Mrs. Camden nodded her head in approval. Angela said "good-bye," then left.

In the hallway outside the classroom door, Angela mentioned to the parents waiting for the next interview that perhaps they should give Mrs. Camden a couple minutes before going in for their interview. Angela felt completely uninformed about her son's progress and needs, but more powerful was the sense of helplessness Angela felt in leaving this teacher in such a fragile emotional state.

Angela felt that Mrs. Camden needed support. She knew, however, that she would not be able to offer it to her. Angela went to the main office and asked to speak to the principal. Angela spoke with the principal and explained that she had just been with Mrs. Camden in a Parent/Teacher interview that did not go smoothly. Angela asked the principal if he would please go down to Mrs. Camden's room and provide her with moral support because she felt Mrs. Camden was in no condition to continue a full day of Parent/Teacher interviews.

The principal explained that Mrs. Camden had not been feeling well lately and that her emotional response might be linked to that. He asked if Angela wanted to talk about the report card with him. Angela conceded that she had great concerns, but that she was not seeking his help with that at this time because Angela felt that Mrs. Camden and she could work that out at their next interview. If Mrs. Camden desired administrative support, it would be her choice, but professionally Angela was simply asking the principal to offer immediate moral support to his staff member. Mrs. Camden's present emotional state and her ability to get through a day of interviews was Angela's only motivation for seeking the principal's involvement.

THE PHONE CALLS AND THE FOLLOWING WEEK

Angela called Mrs. Camden on the next Monday morning to arrange a follow-up interview. Mrs. Camden's voice wavered noticeably and her tone was curt. Mrs. Camden did not know if she and Angela could meet after school as Angela requested. Mrs. Camden quickly informed Angela that the principal would be sitting in on their meeting, and she did not know if Angela's requested time would suit him. Mrs. Camden's tone was direct and short. She called back later that morning to tell Angela that the time she requested would not work, but that she would call the next day to tell Angela when they could meet to deal with all of this.

The next day, Angela received a message from the principal stating that he and Mrs. Camden were free to meet with her at 8:00 AM or 12:00 noon. The principal was aware that Angela was a teacher and would, presumably, understand that these times were not conducive to a teacher's schedule. Angela's initial reaction was that the principal wanted control over this situation. After a number of unsuccessful attempts to talk directly with him, Angela was finally put through to the principal. He did not express concern for Christopher's educational progress. He did not indicate any interest in finding solutions for Angela's concerns. He never mentioned Christopher's name. Rather, he said, he did not have one free afternoon for the remaining two weeks before the Christmas break. Angela acquiesced, gave up her preferred afternoon time, and asked to be accommodated 15 minutes earlier in a morning slot so that she could get to her own school before the morning bell rang. They never spoke about the purpose of the meeting. Angela suspected that his agenda differed from hers.

Concerned with the manner in which Mrs. Camden and the principal were managing their communication with her, Angela also had some concern about the possibility of a change in Mrs. Camden's behavior, in the classroom, toward Christopher. That afternoon, as she does at the end of every day, Angela asked Christopher how his school day went. His response seemed genuine when he announced that everything was great. He continued to share the highlights of his day. He mentioned that he read in front of the entire classroom while Mrs. Camden sat on the floor with the kids and evaluated his reading.

On the next day, Christopher told Angela that he read to both grade-two classrooms. When Angela asked if this was common practice, Christopher informed her that they had never done that before, but that he was chosen because he was being the best listener. He reported that Mrs. Camden didn't evaluate him today. Instead, she stood with the other second-grade teacher and just listened to him read. Angela concluded that Mrs. Camden was getting a closer look at and a second opinion on Christopher's oral reading ability.

THE SECOND PARENT/TEACHER INTERVIEW

The follow-up interview took place a week after the initial one. Around a little table in Christopher's second-grade classroom, Angela sat with Mrs. Camden and the principal. Midway through the 30-minute session, they were joined by the resource teacher. Mrs. Camden avoided eye contact with Angela. The principal asked Angela to express her concerns. Angela focused on the dramatic change in Christopher's grades for performance, effort, ability, skill development, and work habits from last year to this year. To support his learning at home, Angela asked if Mrs. Camden could identify the specific skills and strategies that Christopher was not able to use.

Mrs. Camden spoke in general terms throughout the interview and avoided Angela's question about Christopher's specific skills. Mrs. Camden had writing samples present, and she compared Christopher's work to those she indicated were of 2 quality. As the four people in the meeting looked through Christopher's work samples, there appeared to be very little difference between Christopher's work and the work Mrs. Camden considered to be superior to his. Together, they determined that the majority of Christopher's written work was equivalent to the 2 standard. However, Mrs. Camden had two examples that, after critical scrutiny, could be assessed as 3s. The exercise was painful to Angela, and all she could gather from it was that Mrs. Camden was determined to define Christopher as a 3 student, regardless of his ability.

Angela then asked Mrs. Camden to identify the required math skills Christopher was not using. Mrs. Camden avoided any specific examples. Mrs. Camden informed Angela that Christopher rushes through his work and says he is bored. When Angela asked how Mrs. Camden handled those behaviors, Mrs. Camden looked shaken and had difficulty formulating an answer.

Angela probed again to determine what mathematical skills Christopher was missing. Mrs. Camden stated that Christopher wasn't missing any. Angela referred to the defined grading system on the report card again and asked the principal to clarify it for her. A grade of a 3 indicates that the student understands and applies new concepts to specific learning situations and uses most required skills and strategies appropriately. A grade of a 2 indicates that the student understands and applies new concepts to most learning situations and frequently uses required skills and strategies effectively. The difference between a 3 and a 2 is the attainment and use of all skills. Mrs. Camden had just indicated Christopher was not missing any skills. The principal looked over the definitions. Mrs. Camden interjected and stated that Christopher wasn't applying them. She did not cite any examples. Angela believed that the evidence Mrs. Camden presented did not support her claim, but Angela decided to let it go because she felt she had nowhere to go.

Feeling frustrated by the lack of specific examples she was getting, Angela decided to try, yet again, to narrow in on a specific area of study. Christopher's reading was of great concern to her. As soon as Angela inquired on this topic, Mrs. Camden produced the diagnostic reading tests from early October. She showed everyone in the meeting that at a second-grade level, Christopher scored at the "frustration range" on the first test. A second assessment at the same level came out in the "instructional range." Angela asked why Mrs. Camden thought the two tests came out at such different ability levels. The resource teacher suggested that the results could indicate inconsistency with Christopher's reading. Mrs. Camden thought Christopher might have been uncomfortable with her because it was only her first week with the class as their replacement teacher.

Because the test scores were inconsistent, Angela asked if Mrs. Camden had other assessments upon which she based her mark. Mrs. Camden hesitated; the principal filled the void by speaking generically about the reading assessment. Mrs. Camden then interjected and explained that she assessed Christopher during guided reading groups and informal classroom observations. Angela asked if Mrs. Camden could identify the specific skills Christopher was not using to read text fluently, a performance indicator in which she graded him with a 3. Mrs. Camden said that Christopher reads with no expression. Angela stated her surprise at this.

At home, Christopher uses great expression, appropriately uses predictable phrases and sentence patterns, attends to varied punctuation, and assumes different voices with each character change. Angela acknowledged that her son's reading to her while curled up under the warmth of his bed covers would be a very safe place to explore these skills. Angela asked Mrs. Camden if she would expect dynamic expression from her students when asked to read in front of the entire class like Christopher had done on Monday or if strong expression was only expected in smaller group settings. Before Angela could complete her sentence, Mrs. Camden strongly denied that Christopher had read before the entire class.

In closing, Mrs. Camden informed Angela that Christopher is a strong student and is very close to having 2s in many areas. In fact, she stated that if she were to do the report card in January, she would assign many 2s. Angela wondered to herself how Mrs. Camden could assign grades for work that hasn't been done yet. Angela didn't bother to ask Mrs. Camden that question. She did ask if Mrs. Camden would be comfortable with Angela keeping in regular contact with her over the next grading period to closely monitor Christopher's skill development so that she could support his learning at home. Mrs. Camden provided Angela with her email address. Angela extended her hand to shake Mrs. Camden's, thanked her for her time and left.

On the way out the door, the principal asked Angela if he could have a moment of her time to speak with him in his office on a more personal level. As they made their way down the hallway to his office, they talked lightly about Christmas and the upcoming holidays. Angela anticipated that he wanted to express his concern for Christopher and the situation that had unfolded. Angela thought that the principal would apologize for the lack of concrete examples provided in the interview and for the limited direction provided. Angela thought that he would empathize with her frustration. Angela expected him to tell her that this teacher had little assessment experience, but that they had identified this and were working to support her in this area of growth. Angela imagined him asking if she could be patient and understanding of the process. Angela assumed that he would have been thinking of Christopher first.

Instead, Angela was quickly reminded by the principal to never assume anything. The principal addressed Angela in a neutral tone, but delivered what she thought was an extremely biased message. The principal expressed his disappointment in the way Angela handled herself at the initial interview. He stated that in his four years as an administrator at this school, he had never had a parent situation like this one. He elaborated on the scene Angela caused, how Angela inappropriately addressed a fellow colleague, and how Angela's behavior left Mrs. Camden in such a state that she was unable to complete some of her interviews that day.

The principal informed Angela that Mrs. Camden felt Angela had spoken to her in a condescending manner, that Angela belittled her, and that Angela unprofessionally questioned her teaching and assessment practices. As her colleague, the principal said he felt it was his responsibility to enlighten and warn Angela in this situation. He claimed that Angela treated Mrs. Camden like a little girl.

As Angela sat in complete disbelief, she struggled to collect her thoughts. She thought about Gandhi, and in the smallest way she could identify with him, as she, too, felt unjustly beaten. What would Gandhi do?

Angela mirrored the principal's neutral tone and told the truth. Angela told the principal that the information he just shared with her was secondhand and inaccurate. Angela suggested that his information represented a single perspective, a perspective that was the product of a highly emotional response. Angela covered, in detail, the accounts of the interview from her perspective. The principal appeared to listen, but repeatedly interrupted in defense of his staff member. He restated that Mrs. Camden's perception was that Angela was unreasonable and unprofessional. The principal stated that Angela caused a serious uproar on his staff that day. He also informed Angela that behavior such as this was not what teachers in this neighborhood were accustomed to. Angela felt that she received a strong message that the principal wanted her to stay away from Mrs. Camden and out of his building. Angela believed that the principal was not interested in dealing with proper assessment or with communicating the best ways for her son to learn.

PERCEPTION VERSUS REALITY

Angela believes that Mrs. Camden has unjustly represented her, and she does not know how far the tainted tales about her have traveled throughout the district. The principal alluded to the idea that there were a number of teachers who were upset by Angela's actions. He said that the teachers in his building have lost respect for Angela. Angela believes that any teachers who have previously taught her children know her for who she is and would question the legitimacy of such accusations. Angela does not feel threatened. She reports that she has lost respect for the leader of her son's school.

Nair (1997) states that we lose respect for our leaders if we do not approve of their conduct. Angela believes that this principal clearly made strong judgments without all the facts. She believes that he was drawn into an emotional drama and that he failed to carefully examine the scenario from an intellectual perspective. She believes that this principal did not exhibit all the desired qualities and beliefs she would like to see in the person running her child's school. Accordingly, Angela says that she knows she must expect more of him and that it would be easy for her to overlook his accusations and his disregard for the evaluative practices in his school.

Angela suspects that the principal would like for her to go away, but she desires a higher standard of leadership in her community's school, so she cannot. She believes that she must stay and let her expectations be heard. She expects teachers and administrators to be truthful and she expects them to continually improve their practice. Assessment is an integral part of the instructional cycle and its purpose is to promote continuous learning. Angela's district states that each school must establish appropriate assessment practices to link instruction and evaluation and to facilitate fair and consistent student progress reporting. Her district informs parents that student work samples and relevant information and documentation in support of achievement indicators should be available at Parent/Teacher interviews. As a parent, this was all Angela asked for. She believes that what she wants is the right thing, and that it is in times of personal reflection that her ideals become clear again, when her intellectual response system is not confused by emotions.

Gandhi asked people to reject both physical violence and violence to the spirit. Although she did not intentionally violate Mrs. Camden's spirit, and, perhaps, if examined closely she actually violated her own, Angela does regret that Mrs. Camden experienced such emotional trauma. Angela has selected a special Christmas gift for Mrs. Camden, an angel of peace. Angela says she will take ownership for her own actions, she will be truthful, and she will continue to pursue her ideals of higher standards of education and leadership.

REFLECTION AND DISCUSSION QUESTIONS: PRACTICAL AND PROFESSIONAL ETHICS

1. What professional ethics, if any, do you think Angela violated?
2. What professional ethics, if any, do you think Mrs. Camden violated?
3. What professional ethics, if any, do you think the principal violated?
4. What do you think: Do teachers who are also parents have greater ethical responsibilities toward their own children than toward their colleagues? Or, in other words, do Mama Bear ethics trump professional ethics?
5. How might Downie and Telfer have dealt with this situation?

REFLECTION AND DISCUSSION QUESTIONS: DIFFERENTIATION OF SELF

1. What do you think of the ways that Angela, Mrs. Camden, and the principal managed themselves in this situation?
2. Angela says that she did not intentionally violate Mrs. Camden's spirit. Do intentions, or outcomes, matter more in a situation like this?
3. Angela says the principal appeared to listen, but repeatedly interrupted in defense of his staff member and he restated that Mrs. Camden's perception was that Angela was unreasonable and unprofessional. The principal stated that Angela caused a serious uproar on his staff that day. He also informed Angela that behavior such as this was not what teachers in this neighborhood were accustomed to. Angela says she will take ownership for her actions, that she will be truthful, and that she will continue to pursue her ideals of higher standards of education and leadership. Kerr and Bowen (1988) state that a well-adjusted family unit allows each person his or her own feelings, that healthy interaction is more important than doing what others view as socially appropriate, and that the differentiated person is capable of strong emotions and spontaneity, but also capable of the objectivity that comes with the ability to resist the pull of emotional responses. Describe Angela's, Mrs. Camden's, and the principal's behaviors in this situation that you think either contribute, or do not contribute, to their differentiation of self.

22

Dealing with Backbiting

> I sacrificed my values and beliefs in order to preserve the trust and friendship of two colleagues. My feelings of disappointment stemmed from the fact that I did not interrupt and redirect this conversation to preserve the dignity of the teacher under attack. I did not live up to my own moral beliefs.
>
> Vivian

Nair makes the point that "Most of us reflect on our actions after we recognize that we have hurt someone or done an injustice" (1997, p. 35). Leadership positions within a school provide many opportunities to examine one's values and core belief systems. Recently, Vivian, an experienced teacher who was interested in becoming a principal, was serving as principal designee. She found herself in a situation where she felt that she did not act within the guidelines of her personal belief system. Reflecting on the circumstances, Vivian says she is able to be more objective about the feelings that she experienced then and about how she might handle such situations in the future.

BODY COUNT

The actual student number count at Vivian's school was below what the district had projected. Therefore, the school was required to reassign one teacher to another school. The students had been with their teachers and classmates for three weeks and many bonds were already established, so the decision about which teacher would leave the school was certain to be a difficult one. Based on enrollment numbers, the decision was made to reassign one of the three second-grade teachers. One of them would be asked to go to another school, and the students in her class would then be distributed between the other two second-grade classrooms in the school. Of the three second-grade teachers, two had worked together for years and had developed a solid team-planning approach. The third was new to the building last year and had taught for just one year.

In the effort to operate democratically as a school, the teachers and the principal often made decisions collaboratively. All three second-grade teachers were asked to come together, discuss the situation, and have the opportunity to voluntarily move, should any of them wish a transfer to another school. The hope was that everyone would work together to solve this dilemma. For a variety of complicated professional and personal scheduling reasons, it proved impossible for the three second-grade teachers and the principal to meet at the same time in the compressed time frame.

Due to the short time frame, Vivian was asked by the principal to speak to the two senior teachers in this group while the principal spoke to the third and less-experienced teacher. In discussing the positive and negative aspects of the decision to collapse a grade-two classroom, the two senior teachers began to criticize and denigrate the teaching ability and personality of the younger teacher. Their goal, Vivian suspected, was to impress upon her how well-suited they were to team teaching with each other and how they should be the ones to remain at the school.

VIVIAN'S EMOTIONAL RESPONSE

Vivian reports that her emotional response was one of disbelief and anger. She felt her cheeks flush and her hands clench. She says that her heart started to pound more quickly and she found it difficult to maintain eye contact with the teachers who were speaking. She began to shift in the chair and feel discomfort, both physically and mentally, because these teachers were criticizing a colleague whom she believed had an excellent working relationship with both of them.

As Vivian listened to their comments, she tried to understand their motives and intentions in speaking the way they did. She tried to look at the situation from their perspective. She knew they were speaking to her as a friend and a colleague, not as an administrator. Vivian decided their motives were to preserve the relationship they had with each other, and she believed that they were trying to focus the decision about who should leave based on how well they were teaching, by criticizing the other teacher. Vivian also suspected that they were tired of the time it took to help the newer teacher learn the routines and procedures that were so firmly established in the grade-two programs. Vivian knew they wanted to stay together; however, she also knew that the way they decided to criticize the third teacher was unprofessional.

As the two teachers continued to speak, Vivian began to think of how she should handle the situation. She began to formulate questions that she would ask them and suggestions she would make. All the while, she also thought about how she could control her emotions and not visibly display the anger and disappointment she was feeling. Vivian says that she knew she needed to stop the two teachers from their continued backbiting and redirect their comments and concerns; however, she let them continue to speak while she mentally rehearsed her comments to herself. Vivian says that this is the root of her ethical dilemma: She let the two teachers speak and criticize when she should have immediately redirected and refocused their comments.

VIVIAN'S ACTIONS

Finally, Vivian interrupted the flow of complaints and criticisms. She took a deep breath and calmly asked if they had expressed their concerns to this teacher. When they responded that they had not, Vivian asked them to think about their comments from the point of view of that third teacher. She asked them, "Did you treat her the way you would want to be treated?" They admitted that they should have spoken to her about their concerns, but they were unclear about how to approach her. Vivian asked them if they had tried to include the new teacher into their team. They reiterated their comments about why they should remain at the school and the other teacher should be moved. Their comments indicated that they had spent time talking about the situation, not only among themselves, but with other colleagues, as well. They disclosed that they had asked other teachers for their opinions on who should be reassigned and they shared their comments about why they should remain.

When Vivian asked them to think about the professionalism of their comments, they could find no fault in how they had handled the situation. Vivian knew that if she wanted to be a successful administrator, she would need to put aside her emotions and try to reframe the discussion from one of backbiting to one of solution finding. She highlighted what she knew to be the strengths of the teacher in jeopardy. She also pointed out how new teachers need to have the support of colleagues and, as more experienced teachers, we are the ones in a position to provide support. Vivian asked them to think back to when they were new teachers and were mentored by peers and colleagues. She asked if they realized that, based on her experience, the principal had no idea that these concerns even existed. Vivian asked them to think about the decision, from the principal's point of view, in providing the best for the school. She tried to ask questions in order for the two teachers to think about the bigger perspective and the feelings of the other teacher involved.

FORCES AFFECTING THE SITUATION

Vivian says many different forces contributed to her reactions to the situation. Friendship, for example, played a huge role. Vivian was a close colleague to these teachers. They had each come to her many times to ask for advice on teaching, assessment, classroom management, and how to handle parent concerns. Vivian felt that they had a good professional relationship. Vivian thought they believed that she would listen as a friend and not find fault in the way they chose to handle the situation. Vivian suspects this was why they felt it was acceptable to talk about their colleague in the way they did. They felt comfortable and secure in their friendship with her; they believed she would advocate for them as they tried to preserve their jobs and their teaming situation. They truly believed that by exposing the faults and shortcomings of the third teacher, they were presenting the best case for themselves. Vivian discovered how difficult the role of an administrator could be when dealing with friends and colleagues.

Vivian also discovered that it was difficult for her not to view the situation through her personal lens of what is professional and ethical. She found it difficult not to judge these teachers against her own standards of conduct. Where they felt they were doing the right thing (making themselves look good) for the right reason (to provide the best grade-two program for the students), Vivian felt that they were seeing the situation from their perspective only and were trying to preserve their positions at the expense of the dignity of a colleague.

Vivian's disappointment in the actions of the two teachers came directly from her belief in the fact that more experienced colleagues need to mentor and nurture new teachers in order to boost their confidence and increase their skills. Vivian believes it is wrong to talk about colleagues behind their backs, no matter what the motive. She believes it was unprofessional for these two teachers to have discussed these issues with colleagues and have colleagues take sides in this situation. Vivian realized that there were many perceptions about the same situation, but she believed that this was a private conversation between administration and the grade-two teachers and to discuss it with so many other colleagues showed a breach of professionalism.

Having had the time to reflect on this conversation and her reactions to it, Vivian realized that she sacrificed her values and beliefs in order to preserve the trust and friendship of these two colleagues. She learned a valuable lesson from this interaction as she realized that her feelings of disappointment stemmed not as much from the unprofessional comments of the teachers, but more from the fact that she did not interrupt and redirect this conversation to preserve the dignity of the teacher under attack. Vivian believes she didn't live up to her own moral beliefs.

REFLECTION AND DISCUSSION QUESTIONS: PRACTICAL AND PROFESSIONAL ETHICS

1. Vivian discovered how difficult the role of an administrator could be when dealing with friends and colleagues. How might Hume, Kant, and Gandhi approach the ethics of a person having institutional power over his or her friends?
2. Vivian also discovered that it was difficult for her not to view the situation through her own lens of what is professional and ethical. She found it difficult not to judge these teachers against her own standards of conduct. Is there any way to avoid this?
3. Vivian says she thinks these two teachers believed they were doing the right thing (making themselves look good) for the right reason (to provide the best grade-two program for the students). Draw upon any two theorists to compare and contrast this type of behavior as *doing the right thing for the right reason*.
4. Vivian thought these teachers were trying to preserve their positions at the expense of the dignity of a colleague. Is there anything wrong with that? Examine the issue of self-interest in this case through any of the theoretical lenses in this book to see if you can make a case for this behavior.

REFLECTION AND DISCUSSION QUESTIONS: DIFFERENTIATION OF SELF

1. Vivian says she sacrificed her values and beliefs in order to preserve the trust and friendship of these two colleagues. Describe a situation in which you've gone against your own values to preserve the trust and friendship of others. How did if feel? What did you learn about yourself? How might you have handled it differently?
2. Vivian says she interrupted the flow of complaints and criticisms, took a deep breath, and calmly asked the two teachers if they had expressed their concerns to the other teacher. When they responded that they had not, Vivian asked them to think about their comments from the

point of view of the third teacher. She asked them, "Did you treat her the way you would want to be treated?" Often, when anxiety is high, many people make emotionally based decisions that aren't much more than taking sides. The issue for differentiation of self is to keep a focus on one's own self, but still maintain open and clear communication with the other people involved. Explain your thinking about whether Vivian has accomplished this.

23

An Ethical Use of Sick Days?

I feel that I have moved on in my thinking. I think that I can show respect for my students as individuals by communicating better and by showing my humanness to them. I do not have to be quite as rigid in my work ethic as I once thought I had to be.

Norma

"We all operate from an inner compass, something that guides our decision-making processes. How this compass develops and matures is not always something to which we give a lot of thought. We go through life doing what feels like the right thing. When trying to decide what the right thing to do is, we are sometimes at a loss about what parameters to use to form our decisions. Are we born with this moral compass or is it nurtured and formed as we experience life? A recent experience has helped me recalibrate my moral compass" (Norma).

Norma believes that being raised by parents who survived the Great Depression formed a great deal of her work ethic. Although it was not often discussed in her home, her parents' experience was a fundamental determiner of her family's values. Norma says that in her family, "We were expected always to work as hard as possible and always to do our work until it was complete, not just until our time was up. There was an unspoken belief in our house that it was a privilege to have a job, and whatever the boss said was the way it would be."

THE SITUATION

Norma had always adhered to this concept. In her 20 years as a teacher, she had not taken more than three or four sick days, and her district provided no wellness days in the contract. It was not that she was a martyr; it was more that she takes very good care of her health and that she manages to avoid most of the germs that run rampant throughout a school. However, she also believes that her students need a dependable leader in their classroom, and that they rely on her to be there with the same expectations for them every day. Because of this, Norma had probably neglected her own children on occasion when they were ill or needed her attention.

For example, Norma's husband would take time off from his work to take their children to the orthodontist. The irony of this is that he would then be looked upon as a "good father" for doing so. If Norma had taken the time off from her job as a classroom teacher to do the same thing, she would have violated her contract. But, where his work, primarily paperwork of some sort, would wait for him to come back to the office, Norma's work, her students, would be sitting there, expecting her every day.

A recent decision with which Norma struggled occurred just before her mother's death. Norma's sister called her from out of town, saying that their mother would probably not recover from a relapse that she had suffered. Norma taught the next day and, after school, spent several hours writing up plans for her substitute. Norma then drove to the small town where her mother was hospitalized.

Norma was understandably distraught at the prospect of losing her mother. Norma's mother was the strength and humor that held the family together. Her perfectionism in her sewing and cooking was legendary; she had always been a role model for not only Norma, but for Norma's siblings as well. Just as understandably, Norma was feeling some relief. Her mother suffered from Alzheimer's, and she had been hospitalized for four years. With this relief came guilt at the fact that Norma was not hoping for her mother's survival. She had suffered more than enough in her last few years; Norma did not want it to continue.

Therefore, with Norma's complex array of emotions and her well-entrenched work ethic, it was no surprise that the next day Norma found herself almost apologizing to her principal and offering to return for work the following day if she thought it necessary. It was then that Norma learned an important first lesson: Her principal insisted that she stay. She told Norma that she would never have this time again with her mother and family and to make the most of it. Norma now wonders why someone had to tell her this. But, she has since thought so many times of how right her principal was. Norma and her family ended up having an unforgettable week at their mom's bedside. Although her mom never regained consciousness, Norma and her family spent the week talking, laughing, and making their mom as comfortable as possible. That was the most time they had spent together as a family in over 40 years. Norma is now amazed at how close she was to throwing it away because of an overdeveloped sense of duty.

Norma's second lesson was from her students. Why did Norma think that they couldn't get along without her? She was well planned; her classes were organized down to the last detail, and her substitute teacher was hand-picked. Norma's students were in no danger of missing important information or of being mistreated. What would Norma have been teaching her students if she had let them think that her job came before her family? When Norma returned, she never actually addressed her absence; she keeps her private life out of her professional life. However, her students were aware of why she was gone, and several of them said that they felt sorry for her for why she had to be away. Norma really didn't know what to say to them. She now thinks that she kept too much of an emotional distance between herself and her students. Norma is very interested in, and knowledgeable about, her students' lives; and, in all fairness, Norma now thinks that they need to know a little more about her. Norma has since tried to be a little less private and let her students know that teachers have personal lives. Norma is still a very private person, but she thinks she has a more open and honest relationship with her students as a result of their expressing their concern.

Norma says, "For better or for worse, we take for granted the values we internalized as we grew up and matured. Without being aware of it, we accept these ideas and think that everyone follows the same rules. However, I feel that I have now moved on in my thinking. The changes I have experienced are concurrent with the overall changes that have occurred in our society in the past 30 years. We now believe less in blind obedience to authority. We now expect individuals to make individual decisions. We have come to believe that, in many cases, duty to self supersedes duty to society. This shift in thinking has not always had a positive impact on society, but, in this case, I think that I can show respect for my students as individuals by communicating better and by showing my humanness to them. I do not have to be quite as rigid in my work ethic as I once thought I had to be."

REFLECTION AND DISCUSSION QUESTIONS:
PRACTICAL AND PROFESSIONAL ETHICS

1. Norma has experienced quite a journey in the development of her ethics. She describes internalizing a strong work ethic and an "overdeveloped sense of duty," that "whatever the boss said was the way it

would be," and that she "probably neglected her own children on occasion when they were ill or needed her attention." Of the theorists you've read about, which ones might be most likely to support these ethics? Which ones might be most likely to not support them?

2. Norma said her husband would take time off from his work to take their children to the orthodontist, that the irony of this is that he would then be looked upon as a "good father" for doing so, but that if Norma had taken the time off from her job as a classroom teacher to do the same thing, she would have done something illegal. What is your assessment of the ethicality of this type of situation? What is the status of sick days versus wellness days in the negotiated agreements in your area? What is your assessment of the ethicality of those agreements?

3. Norma describes her complex array of emotions and her well-entrenched work ethic, as she dealt with the logistics of being with her mother on her deathbed. She says it was no surprise she found herself almost apologizing to her principal, offering to return for work the following day if she thought it necessary. Her principal insisted that she stay. She told Norma that she would never have this time again with her mother and family and to make the most of it. Norma now wonders why someone had to tell her this. Norma's district does not have wellness days in the negotiated contract, only sick days. What might Plato or Kant say about the way the principal and Norma handled this? What might Hume or Rand say?

REFLECTION AND DISCUSSION QUESTIONS: DIFFERENTIATION OF SELF

1. Norma asks, "What would I have been teaching my students if I had let them think that my job came before my family?" Describe your boundaries between job and family.

2. "For better or for worse, we take for granted the values we internalized as we grew up and matured. Without being aware of it, we accept these ideas and think that everyone follows the same rules." Norma has described the origins of her values. Can you describe yours?

3. "However, I feel that I have now moved on in my thinking. The changes that I have experienced are concurrent with the overall changes that have occurred in our society in the past 30 years. We now believe less in blind obedience to authority. We now expect individuals to make individual decisions. We have come to believe that, in many cases, duty to self supersedes duty to society." Norma describes the evolution of her thinking and values. Can you describe yours?

24

Who Cares If We Don't Teach Science?

> I've let group-think and a rush to judgment drive my thinking and actions. Blowing a fuse has been an ineffectual problem-solving strategy, so I chose not to repeat that mistake.
>
> Stella

September is always a busy and strenuous month for teachers. Stella was transferred from her Kindergarten teaching position two days into the academic year because the student population did not support a full-time teacher at that level. She was subsequently placed in a third-grade teaching assignment (for which she had no previous training) in the last week of September. Imagine her surprise at being transferred again due to another drop in the student numbers. Stella was then transferred to another school, where her placement would be to team-teach a first- and second-grade combination classroom. That school had been given the designation of a growing school, thus Stella had no reason to fear another transfer for the remainder of the year.

THE SITUATION

Stella's new teaching partner, Ingrid, was young and close to Stella's age. Ingrid was energetic and outgoing. It appeared that Stella and Ingrid shared many of the same likes and dislikes, and Stella looked forward to a good working relationship with Ingrid. As the weeks passed, they established a good working routine.

They began discussing their upcoming units of study and how they might look in the classroom. Because of teaching a combination classroom, their curricular responsibilities were fairly heavy. Classrooms with combined grades will often exclude certain units of study so that they may be covered in the second year of the combination. For example, one half of the first-grade Science units and one half of the second-grade Science units might be explored during year one of the combination, and the remaining units might be covered the following year. This design looked good in theory, but it did not account for pupil transfer, second-grade students who attend the school for only the second year of the combination, or students who have joined the school from a single-grade experience.

Stella and Ingrid had several discussions about how best to explain, explore, and extend these upcoming Science units. Ingrid stated in an offhand manner to Stella that she could "care less if we taught Science because let's face it, Language Arts and Math are more important anyway. If we don't get to it, who cares?" It would be an understatement to say that Stella was surprised by this comment.

Stella doesn't dispute the importance of Language Arts and Math. She believes that they are the center around which many of the core subjects revolve. However, excluding Science altogether seemed very, very wrong to her. Stella also learned that Ingrid's opinion of Social Studies, Health, Physical Education, Computers, and Art were similar to her "outlook" on Science.

STELLA'S EMOTIONAL RESPONSE

Disbelief and dismay dominated Stella's thought processes when Ingrid made this comment. The previous six weeks of her professional life were, at best, a disaster, and she truly did not feel like dealing with this sort of problem. Stella was also feeling somewhat resigned to the situation: She felt that "for some 'cosmic reason' she was being challenged, once again, to overcome an obstacle." Stella was becoming increasingly weary of having her resiliency tested!

STELLA'S INTELLECTUAL RESPONSE

Stella knew it would be a gross understatement to say that this matter was a complete breach of any Teacher's Professional Code of Conduct. The school's, district's, state's, students', and parents' expectations and rights would be compromised if Ingrid's beliefs were carried out. Stella wanted nothing to do with the situation.

STELLA'S ACTIONS

Yet, like a good girl, Stella nodded in agreement with her team-partner and decided to do things her own way. Stella proceeded to include several of these subject area components in her Literacy Block activities and gently persuading her team-partner to do the same.

FORCES AFFECTING THE SITUATION

Though this situation was ethically compromising, Stella says that she did not react in the same manner she would have earlier. Why is that? One factor was that the colleague in question was Stella's team-partner, and Stella respected her. As a result, Stella felt that she had to make an effort to improve the situation for all stakeholders. And though Stella is considered a hothead by most of her friends, she is keenly aware of her mistakes and she looks forward to avoiding them in the future. In short, blowing a fuse has been an ineffectual problem-solving strategy in the past, so Stella chose not to repeat that mistake this time around.

Plus, Stella was tired. Tired of the accounting games and political maneuvering that had been played with her teaching life in September and October, and she did not have the energy to get upset about a situation that was workable. Thankfully, her low energy allowed her to think through several options before deciding what to do. In effect, she avoided the pitfalls of rushing to judgment, and she managed to help create a work environment that suited everybody.

In a previous ethically compromising situation, Stella let group-think and a rush to judgment drive her thinking and actions. That situation could have ruined her professionally. She did not wish to experience a similar heartache again. Also, she really liked her team-partner. She felt that the person and the relationship were worth saving.

They worked through the situation together, and they created several teaching units that incorporated all of the core areas. The students enjoyed the activities, and Stella and her partner were able to cover a broader scope of the curriculum in less time. Stella summarizes her learning in this situation like this: "Werner Heisenberg said that an expert is someone who knows some of the worst mistakes that can be made in his subject and how to avoid them. Although I do not consider myself to be an expert, I am continuing to develop the skills needed to recognize and identify ethically compromising situations, and I hope I am also learning to handle them more professionally. I had better be, because our profession is riddled with ethically complex situations."

REFLECTION AND DISCUSSION QUESTIONS:
PRACTICAL AND PROFESSIONAL ETHICS

1. Given that student numbers drive teaching placements, what do you think of the ethics involved in placing a teacher in a third-grade classroom for which she had no previous training?
2. Ingrid stated in an offhand manner that she could "care less if we taught Science because let's face it, Language Arts and Math are more important anyway. If we don't get to it, who cares?" What do you think of the ethics behind this personal statement? What would you think of the ethics behind this statement if it were to be made by a curriculum director as a result of a community survey?
3. Who gets to decide what is taught and what isn't?
4. Of the theorists you've read in this book, would any of them be uninterested in this question?

REFLECTION AND DISCUSSION QUESTIONS:
DIFFERENTIATION OF SELF

1. Stella says she nodded in agreement with her team-partner and decided to do things her own way. If you have ever avoided conflict this way, how did it work for you?
2. Though this situation was ethically compromising, Stella says that she did not react in the same manner she would have earlier. Describe ways in which you have consciously tried to managing ethically complex situations. How did they work for you?
3. Stella says she is considered a hothead by most of her friends, she is keenly aware of her mistakes, and she looks forward to avoiding them in the future. Stella says blowing a fuse has been an ineffectual problem-solving strategy in the past, so she chose not to repeat that mistake this time around, and she did not have the energy to get upset about a situation that was workable. Is there anything in Stella's story that resonates with you, your experiences, or your goals?

25

Annie's Analysis of Her Professional Ethics

My past has had a tremendously negative impact on me. If I recognize the potential for an argument or even just a discussion of a negative issue, I freeze up. So, naturally, I want to avoid the situation altogether. It is time to become more assertive and stand up for what I believe.

Annie

Growing up, many of us never really consider anyone's perspective except our own. This applies especially to how students view teachers. It is often not until we are actually in a teaching position that we realize that there is a private side to the people (now ourselves) in front of the room. When interacting with fellow teachers, most of us are usually aware that everybody has a story and, of course, we are especially aware of our own. Our past influences our interactions in the workplace, just as other teachers are affected by their life experiences. Knowing all this, we have to decide whether to get involved in teacher-student conflicts to which we are a third party. We want to be fair; we want to do "the right thing for the right reason," but our past can hamper our resolve, so what should we do?

THE SITUATION

Annie's current, yet unresolved, ethical dilemma has been developing for over a year. In essence, it is teacher-student conflict, in which she is caught in the middle. The students are in a program and have had the same math instructor for three semesters. Over the course of this time period, the over-all relationship between the teacher and the students has gradually and continuously deteriorated to the degree that students have angrily yelled out their frustrations in class and left the classroom in protest. How does Annie come into play? Here is how: In January, Annie started tutoring a student who had to retake a failed math final. Of course, Annie talked to the instructor to discover what the course covered and how the tests are structured. When he talked about the student Annie was tutoring, he said in a belittling tone, "Oh well, she is still trying to figure out how to use the calculator." Annie left this remark unanswered even though she thought it disrespectful toward the student. However, this was her first contact with this particular instructor, so she did not want to judge him based on one observation and thought, "Maybe he has a strange sense of humor."

The student passed this make-up final with a B+, but returned for more tutoring during that semester after she failed her third test. Despite the intense tutoring, she received only a Pass on the fourth test. To Annie's shock and dismay, the teacher told her that she should quit the entire program because she would be unsuccessful in math anyway. Annie prevented her from quitting, and she worked with her regularly, with the result that she passed the course with a B+. Although Annie averted this crisis, other little incidents happened, which have made Annie increasingly uncomfortable.

During that spring semester, word of mouth traveled about Annie's tutoring, and 8 out of 21 students in the class attended her review session for the final exam. Despite the review, one student failed the course even though she passed the final. So, once again, Annie prepared that student for a make-up exam. After she wrote it, Annie talked to the instructor again, and he said, "I gave her a C, but she is not going to pass and will have to take both the previous and the current courses again." Annie was shocked and disappointed, but then she thought, "Wait a minute. If she failed before and now has a C as a final grade, then she must have done substantially better on the make-up final since the final exam accounts only for a portion of the final grade." And then Annie thought, "Oh my, here we go again—another student who that so-called teacher thinks won't make it, even though he was so wrong with the first student." By this time, it was the middle of October and another incident occurred about a month later. Annie was talking with one of the students outside when the instructor passed by, then said to Annie: "I will drop the test off for *her* later." Annie could not believe that he was referring to the student, who was standing next to them, in the third person.

Apart from these isolated incidents, the overall situation is not positive, either. After three semesters, some students do not even go to his classes anymore; they prefer to work straight from the textbook. Annie has been conducting regular weekly study sessions (three hours a week), with three to ten students in attendance for each session. The whole situation just snowballed on her—one student had turned into ten students. She feels like she is teaching the class: She teaches them the process involved in recognizing the type of problem before simply pointing to the appropriate formula; she breaks the process of solving a problem into concrete steps; she explains their assignments and practice questions; and she is the one who creates the practice tests. Obviously, time to approach the math teacher is long since overdue; yet, she has not done so.

ANNIE'S INTELLECTUAL RESPONSE

Annie reports that she has been analyzing the problem: Why does the conflict between the students and the instructor exist in the first place? She knows that this particular group is not the easiest group to teach. Their schedule is extremely busy and because they are all in the same classes, once a polarization of opinion occurs, a reversal of that opinion is incredibly difficult. Nevertheless, the motivation to succeed is present. After all, Annie would not have a constant stream of students in her office if the motivation were not there in the first place. Somehow, they make the time to ensure they get the tutoring they need in order to pass the math course. Consequently, Annie believes that the major fault in this case is probably with the math instructor.

This certainly seems to be the case when examining student feedback. Although students' comments have to be appraised cautiously, their remarks are consistently negative. In a review session for example, the teacher waited for students to ask questions. Obviously, he is thinking that it is the students' responsibility to ask for what they do not know, but these students were confused about most basic concepts and were unable to ask appropriate questions. Furthermore, when students did ask him how to solve basic problems, the explanations were just the same as those previously given in the class and still just as unhelpful. In other words, he does not tailor his teaching to the students' particular needs.

Overall, this instructor and Annie have different approaches to, and philosophies of, teaching. His opinion seems to be that potential failure is in fact, probable failure, whereas success is the exception. This attitude is counteracting and undermining students' success. Annie's outlook on teaching is exactly opposite. If someone really wants to learn something and is willing to expend the effort necessary to achieve that outcome, almost anything is possible. Annie knows that there are realistic academic limitations; however, very few students reach these boundaries. Annie has been working at the school for over three years, but she has encountered only one student whose academic goals were beyond her reach.

In addition to analyzing the reasons for the existing conflict, Annie is weighing the advantages and disadvantages of talking to the math teacher, both of which, in her thinking, depend on the outcome of the conversation. If the math teacher reacts positively, the advantages could include a possible improvement of the learning experience for the students. Indirectly, the math teacher may also benefit because teaching may be more rewarding for him. And finally, Annie knows she will feel good about herself because she will have affected positive change not only for a few students in the present, but also for many students in the future and, of course, a colleague.

Conversely, if the math teacher reacts negatively, the disadvantages would include a strained future working relationship with that instructor and possibly an adverse effect for the students. In the worst-case scenario, the math teacher could become vindictive and, in order to prevent Annie's tutoring success, he could create extremely difficult exams. He could even damage Annie's own professional relations in that he is on the union's executive committee. However, overall, the advantages of speaking with the math teacher outweigh the disadvantages because even if he were to react in a retaliatory manner, Annie could always talk to his department head. Logically then, Annie has every reason to address the problem, so why doesn't she?

ANNIE'S EMOTIONAL RESPONSE

The answer to that question lies in her past. Annie grew up in an alcoholic family with emotional and physical abuse, and her coping mechanism was to turn into "the passive, quiet one of the family." She escaped this situation eight years ago when she moved from Germany. At that point, she was extremely insecure despite being the top student all throughout school and extremely shy because she had withdrawn from social contact at the onset of adolescence. She has worked through many of her issues, especially regarding assertiveness and shyness, so much so that at her class reunion, her former classmates could not believe that she was the same person they had come to know in high school. Whatever her progress has been, however, she still experiences a physical panic reaction at any sign of conflict. Hence, she tries to avoid it.

Consequently, she feels completely torn emotionally. On the one hand, she strongly believes that she should talk to the math teacher. Every single time she has contact with the math teacher, she burns with anger and indignation. Not only does she hear, on an almost daily basis, negative comments about his class, but she also has her own negative impressions of him. Any time he talks about students, it is in a derogatory way: They will not make it; they do not have the prerequisite skills to make it; they cannot interpret the wording; they cannot use the calculator—it is always "they can't." Sometimes she just wants to shake him and scream, "Well, then teach them!"

On the other hand, she hates conflict and confrontations. If she recognizes a potential for an argument or even just a discussion of a negative issue, she freezes up; in fact, her mind goes literally blank, so, naturally, she wants to avoid the situation altogether. She is skilled at resolving other people's conflicts, but this is one of her own. Judging from the math teacher's behavior, Annie believes that he thinks there isn't an issue; in fact, it seems that any class conflict is categorized and dismissed as a "student-problem," not a "teacher-problem." Annie is essentially the one who has a problem with how the math teacher treats his students and how he runs his class, but who gives her the right to interfere? Annie wants to see what different philosophers would do in this case.

ANNIE'S ANALYSIS

Plato

Plato judged the ethicality of an action using two principles: first, was harm done or not, and second, was the law followed or not. In this case, no particular law is telling Annie whether to confront the instructor or not. The only unwritten law that exists is that any conflict should be attempted to be resolved with the instructor first, before taking the issue further up the administrative chain. This is a practice with which Annie wholeheartedly agrees, even though it would be much easier for her to talk to the department head because, in doing so, she would circumvent a direct confrontation with the math teacher.

Regarding the first principle, Plato considered any action that causes harm to another person to be unjust and unethical. Is there any future harm in Annie's actions? There could be if the math teacher turns vindictive, but then it would be he who would be acting unjustly and unethically. Nevertheless, Annie would feel responsible on an emotional level even if she could rationalize a negative outcome. However, if he were receptive to Annie's suggestions about teaching, then the benefits would be tremendous— as outlined in her intellectual response above. Evidently, according to Plato, Annie should act, especially when she takes into account that Plato considered cowardice as one of the greatest evils, which corrupts the soul.

Hume

According to Hume, ethical judgments are, in essence, judgments of sentiment. Consequently, the ethical dilemma Annie is feeling is a result of the different philosophies between herself and the math teacher. Although the math teacher seems to be comfortable with his behavior as a teacher, Annie judges his attitudes and actions as unethical. However, she cannot stop here: Even though Hume sees ethicality as a private judgment, Hume would not judge the math teacher's actions as virtuous because "virtues were traits that were either useful or agreeable, or both, to one's self, others, or both" (1751/1983, p. 6). After all, this math teacher's attitude toward the students tends to be neither useful for them nor agreeable to them.

Furthermore, Hume proposes that justice is based on community moral values, and, as a result, must emerge out of shared community values. Obviously, the shared community is the community of students and teachers, and this teacher certainly does not uphold its values. An educational institution is supposed to help students succeed, but Annie's perception and experience is that this math teacher discourages students and does not adapt his teaching style, for example, by explaining concepts in an alternative fashion when asked for it.

Should Annie act? Hume argued that the ethicality of a decision is based on the outcome, but Annie does not know what the outcome will be. Nevertheless, not knowing the outcome does not excuse inactivity; Annie thinks that perhaps she should act with prudence and positive regard toward the future. Talking to the math teacher would accomplish just that. In other words, according to Hume, Annie should act, as well.

Kant

Kant stressed two widely accepted principles of morality: universal rules and respect. In other words, moral rules have to apply to everybody (there should be no double standard), and people should be treated as ends in themselves, not as means. By approaching the math teacher, Annie would uphold both principles. She believes that suggestions for improvement should be communicated, even when they entail criticism about effectiveness. For example, years ago in grade school, when Annie's fifth-grade math teacher asked her to tutor a classmate, Annie was devastated when other children in the class told her that her tutee did not find the sessions helpful. During the next session, Annie asked what the problems were, and then she and the tutee adjusted the tutoring accordingly. Annie treated this student as an end in himself; Annie wanted him to succeed. Similarly, in her current ethical dilemma, Annie wants the math teacher and his students to have a better, more constructive relationship; in this respect, she is treating them as ends in themselves.

Kant expresses these two principles in his categorical imperative: "There is therefore but one categorical imperative, namely, this: Act only on that maxim whereby thou canst at the same time will that it should become a universal law" (1785/1981, p. 112). The question Annie then needs to ask herself is, "What if everybody did what I am proposing to do?" The result would be honesty—which could backfire, depending on how criticism is delivered. Because her goal is to improve the situation, she would approach the subject very nonconfrontationally and constructively. Consequently, if criticism were delivered respectfully, she would want others to act the way she intends to act.

In this respect, Kant would not agonize over the possible outcomes; he says, "the moral worth of an action does not lie in the effect expected from it, nor in any principle of action which requires to borrow its motive from the expected effect" (p. 109). In other words, it does not matter if Annie will be successful when talking to the instructor or if the situation for the students becomes worse. As a result, Annie should act because her motives are ethical and the consequences are irrelevant to determining her duty; Annie will simply have to follow her conscience.

Mill

Opposite to Kant, who focused on motives as the criteria of ethicality, Mill focused on the outcome: one should produce good consequences and avoid evil ones, striving for the "greatest happiness for the greatest number of people"—the essence of Utilitarianism. That, in itself, is a noble concept, especially when considering that when we estimate the greatest common good from various actions, personal interests and the interests of others should be assessed objectively.

However, how does Annie assess all interests objectively? How does she measure positive and negative consequences in order to decide whether her decision will have utility or benefit? She could assign her own discomfort a "–10" and each student's positive outcome a "+1," but she does not know what the result will be. Nevertheless, in the best case scenario, the students, the teacher, and Annie would benefit, so Mill would act in her circumstances as well, especially when considering that "he contended that the ultimate sanction 'of all morality is a subjective feeling in our minds'" (1861/ 1979, p. 18), and Annie certainly feels that her motives are ethical.

Downie and Telfer

Annie wholeheartedly believes in Downie and Telfer's approach to the situation, which can be summarized as: Respect for persons is the single fundamental principle from which all rules of ethics are derived. Annie's motives are derived from respect for the students. Conversely, she feels that the math teacher has disrespected his students, and this, in itself, demands that Annie take action. However, Downie and Telfer (1909) stressed the duties of private morality; Annie should develop her own nature and natural talents. If she has not completely developed her conflict resolution skills, Annie owes it to herself to develop those skills; but, it is not necessarily a moral flaw if she does not act on her duty toward others until she is ready to do so. In fact, Downie and Telfer point out that because both duty to self and duty to others are binding, one must choose between the two. Consequently, Annie could rationalize inaction, but in order to develop conflict resolution skills, she cannot consistently avoid conflict; she would not learn how to resolve conflicts, just like one does not learn how to ride a bike without getting on a bike. As a result, Annie should act because the outcomes could be positive for others and for her own self.

Gandhi

Gandhi committed himself to truth and nonviolence—the absolute values by which to live one's life. Annie believes that the math teacher violates the concept of nonviolence because, for Gandhi, nonviolence is not just a rejection of violence; it is the positive love for all humanity; therefore, violence includes all forms of exploitation including discrimination. In a sense, the math teacher is discriminating against the students, especially his female students, by categorizing them as incapable right from the start. As soon as that happens, discrimination and prejudice will influence one's actions, as they do in this case. Annie is positive that the instructor is not even aware of his derogatory remarks and their effect on the students.

However, Gandhi went beyond simply committing himself to the absolute values privately; he believed in exposing injustices through action. Consequently, even nonviolence demands action. Therefore, Annie should do what is right, as well as not submit to what she knows is wrong. This leads her back to Plato, who considered cowardice as a corruption of the soul. Similarly, "In the end, it is moral courage that determines the standard of leadership in the practical arenas of politics, business, academics, and the community" (Nair, 1997, p. 49). Gandhi lived by his actions, so, of course, if he were to give Annie advice on whether she should take action, he would say, "Absolutely!"

Rand

Rand's Objectivism is based on the assumption that reason is our only way of attaining knowledge. Because of this, Rand rejects mysticism and religion because they have based their morality on some higher standard of good that has been handed down. Consequently, Rand would reject all previously discussed philosophical reasons for what action Annie should pursue in her ethical dilemma.

Nevertheless, even according to Rand, Annie should take action. Rand believed that one's moral responsibility is to one's self. In fact, she states, "The achievement of his own happiness is man's highest moral purpose." So should Annie just do whatever makes her happy? Annie could just tell herself that she should not interfere with this particular class's problem with their teacher, but Rand does not view happiness in such simplistic terms. Happiness comes from self-actualization, and it is up to each individual to determine the values necessary to live life to its highest realization. In order to achieve to her highest realization, Annie has to overcome her fear of conflict. Therefore, she should confront the math teacher, but not because of the positive outcomes it will have for the students. Instead, she should do it so that she overcomes her behavior of avoiding conflict at all costs.

Even though Rand does not condone decisions based on emotion, and inactivity in this instance would certainly be an emotional reaction, she makes a concession: Rand argued that unless one can reason, through logic, that feelings are rational, the feelings must be dismissed. In Annie's case then, the emotions that she feels have a valid reason behind them—her past. As a result, even Rand, who advocated personal choice and freedom and who mistrusted emotions, would tell Annie to act, thereby joining every single philosopher discussed here.

ANNIE'S ACTION PLAN

Here is what Annie plans to do. First of all, she will not proceed until the beginning of the next semester. Right now is a highly stressful time for teachers: grading papers, creating final exams, grading final exams, and getting materials ready for the next semester, not to mention the stress that comes with the holiday season. Hardly any teacher will be in the right frame of mind to listen to criticism, even if it is constructive.

Second, because confronting this math teacher will be such a huge personal task for her, Annie has to be absolutely sure that the problem is really as severe as she thinks it is. That is why she has decided to listen in on his class. It seems sneaky, but before she talks to him about his teaching style and attitude, she has to obtain some first-hand experience. Annie feels justified in this action because, ultimately, her goal is not only to help the students but also the math teacher himself. A few students have indicated that they will complain to his department head as well as the principal of the school, so perhaps her intervention could prevent this problem from escalating to this level, thereby helping the math teacher, as well.

Finally, Annie has been invited to give a 15-minute presentation at the next department meeting at the beginning of the next semester. This will give her the opportunity to address poor teaching practices without addressing any teacher, in particular. Fifteen minutes will not allow her to be as in-depth as she wishes she could be, but maybe the math teacher's interest will be sparked and maybe he will initiate a dialogue. So, Annie will definitely talk with the math instructor, but she will wait until after her presentation to the department.

ANNIE'S CONCLUSION

After having analyzed the situation in light of different philosophical theories, Annie has to conclude that the evidence overwhelmingly points to her taking action. Overall, Annie has recognized that ethically compromising situations arise quickly, that she is very analytical when resolving ethical dilemmas probably because of her sensitivity to conflict, and that her personal ethics are a combination of the different philosophies. Also, when making a decision, Annie tries to follow these three basic principles for ethical decision making: (1) When considering her motives and possible outcomes, she always tries to be fair to all parties involved, (2) She tries to keep her promises, and (3) She tries not to do harm. That does not mean that she has never lied or that she has never hurt anybody. However, neither was the result of spite, disrespect, or malice. Whatever actions she chose seemed to be the most ethical pursuits at the time.

Annie has also learned of the difficulty in following the "golden rule": Do unto others as you would have them do unto you. Simple actions, such as returning a wallet without taking anything or helping someone carry something are easy. What is difficult, however, is asserting herself—confronting injustices she recognizes. In that respect, Annie's past has had a tremendously negative impact on her. She knows it is time to become more assertive and stand up for what she believes. Talking to the math teacher would accomplish just that and bring her one step closer to overcoming her demons—one step closer to freeing herself from her past and moving toward greater happiness, greater self-satisfaction, and maybe a more harmonious state of being.

REFLECTION AND DISCUSSION QUESTIONS:
PRACTICAL AND PROFESSIONAL ETHICS

1. Explain why you do or do not agree with any or all parts of Annie's analyses of her situation.
2. Because confronting the math teacher would be such a huge personal task for Annie, she believes she has to be absolutely sure that the prob-

lem is really as severe as she thinks it is. That is why she decided to listen in on his class. She says, "It seems sneaky, but before I talk to him about his teaching style and attitude, I have to obtain some first-hand experience." What do you think? Is it sneaky to observe a colleague for reasons other than those you would tell the person? Which of the theorists might, or might not, condone a plan that contained a hidden motive?

REFLECTION AND DISCUSSION QUESTION: DIFFERENTIATION OF SELF

1. Annie says it is difficult for her to assert herself, to confront injustices, and that her past has had a tremendously negative impact on her, but that it is time to become more assertive and stand up for what she believes. Talking to the math teacher would accomplish just that, she says, and would bring her one step closer to overcoming her demons, one step closer to freeing herself from her past and moving toward greater happiness, greater self-satisfaction, and maybe a more harmonious state of being. Is there anything in Annie's story that resonates with you, your experiences, or your goals?

26

Welcome to the Journey

Do not wait for leaders; do it alone, person-to-person.

Mother Teresa

As stated in the introduction, the purpose of this book on ethical decision making is not to illustrate the difference between right and wrong, but to show how teachers might choose among ethical approaches to decision making as they face the difficult choices they make every day. After reading the seven chapters on philosophically different approaches to ethics, after examining the emotional aspects of your responses in stressful and anxious times, after reading the 16 chapters that highlight the array of difficult and ethically complex situations teachers face every day, and after reflecting on and discussing the various questions at the end of each chapter, you probably now have a deeper understanding of what justice, fairness, and ethics are, and about how they apply to your professional life.

What is fair? What is just? What are ethics? What is ethical? All of the chapters in this book, up to this point, have been aimed toward helping you make those important decisions for yourself and for your life. But you might be asking yourself at this point, "How do I start?"

How do you start? By doing the reading and thinking so far, you already have. You can also continue developing your understanding of, and thinking behind, your own ethical decision making. You can examine every-day occurrences for their ethical content. You can model what you want to see and hear in your building and classroom.

Knowing that the language and tone you use in meetings, hallways, and private conversations generates other conversations among colleagues and students, you can put into words the thinking behind your own ethical decision making. You can use current examples of both positive and negative situations that engage you in the complexities of ethical decision making. You can make the discussion of ethics a regular topic of conversation among colleagues.

Nair says, "We need a new heroic ideal: the brave, truthful individual who is in the service of humanity, resists injustice and exploitation, and leads by appealing to our ideals and our spirit" (1997, p. 8). When we include ethical criteria in our professional practice, we make a commitment to live to our highest ideals. You can talk about the people who have helped you develop your high standards of leadership. You can be that person.

What happens when we face difficult options? Examining ourselves and why we do what we do is the very essence of ethics. Many of us can look back at different situations and ask ourselves, "Why didn't somebody do something?" Asking ourselves this question helps us recognize that we are the ones who can say or do something.

You can continue to define and articulate your ethical principles. Spitzer (2000) points out that if we do not have any ethical principles to draw upon, then we are reduced to ethics based on the emotions and whims of the moment. Given our ability to rationalize our desires and behaviors, these kinds of ethics simply become our justifications of what is convenient for us to do, especially in difficult circumstances when we are dealing with other people and their ethics.

We rarely know other people's ethics, so in difficult circumstances, it can be helpful to begin an ethical conversation on the three principles common to every ethical base and religion. These three principles that can help us begin an ethical conversation are to follow the Silver Rule, keep your promises, and be fair. We can also know ourselves.

FOLLOW THE SILVER RULE

When we follow the Silver Rule, we do not do unto others what we would not have them do unto us. Even though the Golden Rule presumes the Silver Rule, we should live up to the Silver Rule because we need this rule to be counted on and to be able to count on others.

KEEP YOUR PROMISES

Another principle common to every ethical base and religion is to keep our promises. We are our word. Our word is our life. When we talk about keeping our promises, it is helpful to point out that there are two types of promises: implicit promises and explicit promises. Implicit promises are any moral norm the majority expects, such as: Do not lie, cheat, steal, or do unnecessary harm. Rationalizations don't work with implicit promises; we know that wrong is wrong. Explicit promises are those promises that are fully expressed, such as contractual obligations. We know what people think if we back out of these.

BE FAIR

A third principle common to all ethical bases and religions is to be fair. We know "fair" is a highly subjective word, so we have to ask, 'What does 'fair' mean? We have to define the word in the context it is being used. We can do this by asking what the other person means by fair.' The way Spitzer puts it is, "we have to find out where their resentment level is about the issue" (2000, p. 219). We must do this for at least two reasons. One reason is that we are all very good at rationalizing *our* meaning to include or exclude whatever best meets our needs. The second reason is that we do not want to be the instigators of the cortisol cascade; we know it is not in our, or anyone's, best interest to cause fear or anger due to the other person's sense of what is fair being violated through our actions or our rationalizations.

KNOW YOURSELF

You have read about the sources of ethics of the various philosophers, ranging from justice and the law, sentiment and self-interest, reason and good will, the greatest good for the greatest number, truth and nonviolence, reason and self-interest, and respect for persons. You've thought about and discussed how these different ethical principles compare and contrast with each other and how they might lead to different decisions about a wide array of societal, school based, and personal issues.

Now you can ask yourself, "What is the source of *my* ethics? How is my thinking different from, or similar to, Plato's, or Kant's, or Mill's?" Now that you can define and articulate your ethical principles, you will not be limited to rationalizing desires and behaviors based on justification of what is convenient to do. Now that you can understand what acting on your ethical principles will look like and feel like, you will not be limited to ethics based on the emotions and whims of the moment.

Because the tone of classrooms and schools has profound effects on the experiences of the people who learn, teach, and work there, the standard of a teacher's ethical behavior should fulfill the highest expectations of our students and their parents, our colleagues, and our public. Especially in difficult circumstances, when you are dealing with other people and their ethics, your self-knowledge will help you live up to your own high standards. Welcome to the journey.

REFLECTION AND DISCUSSION QUESTIONS: PRACTICAL AND PROFESSIONAL ETHICS

1. How do I define what justice is?
2. What is my responsibility for my students' well-being?
3. What are my boundaries around work and home?
4. What are my responsibilities for effective self-care?
5. What are my natural talents? How am I developing them?
6. What are my ethics? Where did I get them?
7. Are my actions congruent with my ethics?
8. As a classroom teacher, what kinds of power do I have? Do I ever abuse my power?
9. Are there issues at school about which someone needs to say or do something?
10. Are there issues at school I avoid taking on because I don't want to make waves?

Bibliography

Argyris, C. 1986. Skilled incompetence. *Harvard Business Review* (Sept-Oct): 74–79.

Baker-Miller, J. 1976. Domination-subordination. In *Toward a new psychology of women*, pp. 3–12. Boston: Beacon Press.

Baldwin, J. 1952. *Go tell it on the mountain*. New York: Doubleday.

Bandura, A. 1977. *Social learning theory*. Englewood Cliffs, NJ: Prentice-Hall.

Bass, B. 1990. *Bass and Stogdill's handbook of leadership*. New York: The Free Press.

Black, H. C. 1991. *Black's law dictionary*, abridged 6th ed. St. Paul: West Publishing Company.

Bloom, B. S. 1953. Thought processes in lectures and discussions. *Journal of General Education* 7: 160–169.

Bok, S. 1979. *Lying: Moral choice in public and private life*. New York: Vintage.

Bok, S. 1982. *Secrets*. New York: Pantheon.

Bolman, L. G., and Deal, T. E. 1991. *Reframing organizations: Artistry, choice, and leadership*. San Francisco: Jossey-Bass.

Bondurant, J. V. 1965. *Conquest of violence: The Gandhian philosophy of conflict*. Los Angeles: University of California Press.

Bowen, M. 1978. *Family therapy in clinical practice*. New York: Jason Aronson, Inc.

Branden, B. 1986. *The passion of Ayn Rand*. New York: Doubleday and Co.

Branden, N. 1984. Benefits and hazards of the philosophy of Ayn Rand. *Journal of Humanistic Psychology* 24(94): 39–64.

Brandt, D. R., Miller, G. R., and Hocking, J. E. 1980a. Effects of self-monitoring and familiarity on deception detection. *Communication Quarterly* 28: 3–10.

Brandt, D. R., Miller, G. R., and Hocking, J. E. 1980b. The truth deception attribution: Effects of familiarity on the ability of observers to detect deception. *Human Communication Research* 6: 99–110.

Brandt, D. R., Miller, G. R., and Hocking, J. E. 1982. Familiarity and lie detection: A replication and extension. *Western Journal of Speech Communication* 46: 276–290.

Brown, C. 1963. *Manchild in the promised land*. New York: Signet.

Burns, J. M. 1978. *Leadership*. New York: Harper and Row.

Camden, C., Motley, M. T., and Wilson, A. 1984. White lies in Interpersonal communication. *Western Journal of Speech Communication* 48(4): 309–325.

Cameron, J. K. 2001. Trauma in human systems: a brief introduction. Paper presented to the Los Angeles Unified School District, Los Angeles, CA.

Cameron, J. K. 2004. Traumatic event systems model and threat assessment. Handout presented at the Southern Alberta Teachers' Conference, February Calgary, AB.

Deigh, J. 1992. *Ethics and personality: Essays in moral psychology*. Chicago: University of Chicago Press.

Downie, R. S., Loudfoot, E., and Telfer, E. 1974. *Education and personal relationships*. London: Methuen and Co.

Downie, R. S., and Telfer, E. 1969. *Respect for persons*. London: Allen and Unwin.

Eck, M. 1970. *Lies and truth*. London: Collier-Macmillan.

Ekman, P. 1992. *Telling lies: Clues to deceit in the marketplace, politics, and marriage*. New York: W. W. Norton.

Ekman, P., and Friesen, W. V. 1974. Detecting deception from the body or face. *Journal of Personality and Social Psychology* 20: 288–298.

Etzioni, A. 1988. *The moral dimension: Toward a new economics*. New York: Free Press.

Fisher, L. 1954. *Gandhi: His life and message for the world*. New York: Penguin Books.

Frank, R. H. 1988. *Passions within reason: The strategic role of the emotions*. New York: W. W. Norton.

Frankfurt, H. G. 2005. *On Bullshit*. Princeton, NJ: Princeton University Press.

Friedman, E. H. 1985. *Generation to generation: Family process in church and synagogue*. New York: The Guilford Press.

Friedman, E. H. 1999. *A failure of nerve: Leadership in the age of the quick fix*. Bethesda, MD: The Edwin Friedman Estate Trust.

Frohlich, N., and Oppenheimer, J. A. 1992. *Choosing justice: An experimental approach to ethical theory*. Berkeley: University of California Press.

Gandhi, M. K. 1999. *All men are brothers*. New York: Continuum (First published by UNESCO, 1958).

Gandhi, M. K. 2001. *An autobiography*. London: Penguin Books (First published in Gujarati and in English by the Navajivan Publishing House, 1927).

Gilbert, R. 1992. *Extraordinary relationships: A new way of thinking about human Interactions*. New York: John Wiley & Sons.

Greenleaf, R. S. 1973. *The servant as leader*. Petersborough, NH: Center for Applied Sciences.

Greenleaf, R. S. 1977. *Servant leadership*. New York: Paulist Press.

Hamburg, D. A. 1992. *Today's children: Creating a future for a generation in crisis*. New York: Random House.

Helgesen, S. 1990. *The female advantage*. New York: Doubleday.

Hoefnagels, C., and Zwikker, M. 2001. The bystander dilemma and child abuse: Extending the Latane and Darley model to domestic violence. *Journal of Applied Social Psychology* 31(6): 1158–1183.

Hume, D. 1983. *An enquiry concerning the principles of morals*. Indianapolis: Hackett Publishing Company (Original work published 1751).

Hurston, Z. N. 1990. *Their eyes were watching God*. New York: Harper and Row.

Juergensmeyer, M. 1986. *Fighting fair.* San Francisco: Harper and Row.

Kant, I. 1981. *Grounding for the metaphysics of morals.* J. W. Ellington, trans. Indianapolis: Hackett Publishing Company (Original work published 1785).

Kerr, M. E., and Bowen, M. 1988. *Family evaluation.* New York: W. W. Norton.

Kets de Vries, M. F. R. 1991. *Organizations on the couch: Clinical perspectives on organizational behavior and change.* San Francisco: Jossey-Bass.

Kilmann, R. H., and Saxton, M. J. (1983). *Organizational cultures: Their assessment and change.* San Francisco: Jossey-Bass.

Kimbrough, R. B. 1985. *Ethics: A course of study for educational leaders.* Arlington, VA: The American Association of School Administrators.

Klicker, R. L. 2000. *A student dies, a school mourns. Dealing with death and loss in the school community.* Great Britain: Brunner-Routledge.

Kohlberg, L. 1976. Moral stages and moralization: The cognitive-developmental approach. In *Moral development and behavior: Theory, Research and social issues,* ed. T. Lickona. New York: Holt, Rinehart and Winston.

Kytle, C. 1982. *Gandhi: Soldier of nonviolence.* New York: Everest House.

LaBier, D. 1986. *Modern madness: The emotional fallout of success.* Reading, MA: Addison-Wesley.

Lasswell, H. 1958. *Politics: Who gets what, when, and how.* Cleveland: Meridian Books.

Lepage, M. A. 1993. *The Kafkesque organization.* Available at: http://qlink.queensu.ca/~3mal5/kafkesque.html.

Lerner, A. W., and Wanat, J. 1983. Fuzziness and bureaucracy. *Public Administrator Review* 43(6): 500–509.

Lessler, J., and Tourangeau, R. 1989. Questionnaire design in the cognitive research laboratory. *Vital and Health Statistics* 6: 1.

Levinson, D. J. 1978. *The seasons of a man's life.* New York: Knopf.

Machiavelli, N. 1966. *The prince.* New York: Bantam Books (Original work published 1513).

Mahoney, D. J. 2006. *Balancing the complex demands on school administrators: Understanding the organizational dynamics of the 21st century.* Lanham, MD: Rowman & Littlefield.

McCrosky, J. C. 1966. Scales for the measurement of ethos. *Speech Monographs* 33: 65–72.

Merriam-Webster. 1987. *Webster's ninth new collegiate dictionary.* Springfield, MA: Merriam-Webster.

Milgram, S. 1974. *Obedience to authority: An experimental view.* New York: Harper and Row.

Mill, J. S. 1979. *Utilitarianism.* Indianapolis: Hackett Publishing Company (Original work published 1861).

Mintzberg, H. 1983. *Power in and around organizations.* Englewood Cliffs, NJ: Prentice Hall.

Morgan, G. 1986. *Images of organization.* Newbury Park, CA: Sage Publications.

Nair, K. 1997. *A higher standard of leadership: Lessons from the life of Gandhi.* San Francisco: Berrett-Koehler Publishers.

Nichols, M., and Schwartz, R. 1998. *Family therapy: Concepts and methods.* Boston: Allyn and Bacon.

Norman, R. 1983. *The moral philosophers.* New York: Oxford University Press.

Northouse, P. G. 2001. *Leadership: Theory and practice,* 2nd ed. Thousand Oaks, CA: Sage.

Nyberg, D. 1987. The moral complexity of deception. In D. A. & B. Arnstine (Eds.), *Philosophy of Education, 1987,* pp. 239–252. Normal, IL: The Philosophy of Education Society.

Nyberg, D. 1993. *The varnished truth.* Chicago: University of Chicago Press.

Palmer, P. 2000. *Let your life speak.* San Francisco: Jossey-Bass.

Plato. 1974. *Plato's republic,* G. M. A. Grube, trans. Indianapolis: Hackett Publishing Co (Original work published 380 BC).

Plato. 1987. *Gorgias,* D. J. Zeyl, trans. Indianapolis: Hackett Publishing Company (Original work published 385 BC).

Putnam, L. L., and Mumby, D. K. 1993. Organizations, emotion and the myth of rationality. In *Emotion in organizations,* S. Fineman, ed., pp. 36–57. Newbury Park, CA: Sage.

Rand, A. 1957. *Atlas shrugged.* New York: Signet.

Rand, A. 1961. *The virtue of selfishness.* New York: Signet.

Rand, A. 1962. Introducing objectivism. *The Objectivist Newsletter* 1(8). New York: Objectivist Newsletter Inc.

Ravitch, D. 2000. *Left back: A century of failed school reforms.* New York: Simon & Schuster.

Sapolsky, R. 2005. *Biology and human behavior.* Chantilly, VA: The Teaching Company.

Sarason, S. 1972. Socialization of the leader. In *The creation of settings and future societies,* S. Sarason, ed., pp. 181–215. San Francisco: Jossey-Bass.

Sarason, S. 2002. *Educational reform: A self-scrutinizing memoir.* New York: Teachers College Press.

Schein, E. H. 1985. *Organizational culture and leadership.* San Francisco: Jossey-Bass.

Schwartz, H. S. 1990. *Narcissistic process and corporate decay: The theory of the organization ideal.* New York & London: New York University Press.

Seech, Z. 1988. *Logic in everyday life: Practical reasoning skills.* Belmont, CA: Wadsworth Publishing Co.

Senge, P. M. 1990. *The fifth discipline.* New York: Doubleday/Currency.

Shulman, L. S., and Elstein, A. S. 1975. Studies of problem solving, judgment, and decision making: Implications for educational research. In *Review of research in education,* F. N. Kerlinger, ed., vol. 3. Itasca, IL: Peacock.

Skinner, B. F. 1938. *The behavior of organisms.* New York: Appleton-Century-Crofts.

Skinner, B. F. 1953. *Science and human behavior.* New York: The Free Press.

Skinner, B. F. 1957. The experimental analysis of behavior. *American Scientist* 45: 343–371.

Skinner, B. F. 1959. *Cumulative record.* New York: Appleton-Century-Crofts.

Skinner, B. F. 1963. Behaviorism at fifty. *Science* 140: 951–958.

Smircich, L. 1985. Is the concept of culture a paradigm for understanding organizations and ourselves? In *Organizational Culture,* P. G. Frost, et al., eds., pp. 55–72. Beverly Hills: Sage.

Solomon, R. C. 1992. *Ethics and excellence: Cooperation and integrity in business.* New York: Oxford University Press.

Sorenson, G. 2002. *An intellectual history of leadership studies.* James MacGregor Burns Academy of Leadership, University of Maryland. Available at: http://www.academy .umd.edu/scholarship/casl/articles/sorenson_apsa.htm.

Spitzer, R. 2000. *The spirit of leadership.* Provo, UT: Executive Excellence Publishing.

Sterba, J. P. 1991. *Morality in practice,* 3rd ed. Belmont, CA: Wadsworth Publishing Co.

Stone, D. A. 1988. *Policy, paradox, and political reason.* New York: HarperCollins.

Sullivan, E. 2001. *The concise book of lying.* New York: Picador.

Swenson, R. A. 2004. *Margin: Restoring emotional, physical, financial, and time reserves to overloaded lives.* Colorado Springs, CO: NavPress.

Thompson, C. M. 2000. *The congruent life: Following the inward path to fulfilling work and inspired leadership.* San Francisco: Jossey-Bass.

Titelman, P. 1988. *Clinical applications of Bowen Family Systems Theory.* New York: Haworth Press.

Toulmin, S. 1972. *Human understanding: The collective use and evolution of concepts.* Princeton, NJ: Princeton University Press.

Tuckman, B. W. 1965. Developmental sequence in small groups. *Psychological Bulletin* 63: 384–399.

Weber, M. 1947. *The theory of social and economic organization,* T. Parsons, trans. New York: Free Press (Original work published 1927).

Weiner, B. 1979. A theory of motivation for some classroom experiences. *Journal of Educational Psychology* 71: 3–25.

Weiner, B. 1980. A cognitive (attribution)-emotion-action model of motivated behavior: An analysis of judgments of help-giving. *Journal of Personality and Social Psychology* 39: 186–200.

Weiner, B. 1986. *An attributional theory of motivation and emotion.* New York: Springer Verlag.

Weston, A. 2000. *A rulebook for arguments,* 3rd ed. Indianapolis: Hackett Publishing Company.

Whaley, B. 1982. Toward a general theory of deception. *Journal of Strategic Studies* 5: 185–192.

Wright, R. 1936. *Uncle Tom's children.* New York: Harper and Row.

X, M. 1964. *The autobiography of Malcolm X.* New York: Grove Press.

Zubay, B., and Soltis, J. F. 2005. *Creating the ethical school.* New York: Teachers College Press.

About the Author

Dan Mahoney earned his B.A. at the Evergreen State College in Olympia, Washington, and began teaching in 1978. He is now a professor at Gonzaga, where he teaches courses in ethics, research, educational evaluation, and curricular design. He has served as the editor of *Curriculum in Context* and currently serves on the editorial board of the *Journal of Ethics in Leadership*. He has authored the books *An Organizational Analysis of School Administrators' Use of Deception*, and *Ethics and the School Administrator*, and he has co-authored, with Albert H. Fein, Ph.D., the book *Cracks and Collapse: Issues Facing Teachers and Administrators in the K-12 System*. Dan and his wife, Scooter, live in Spokane, Washington.